TOUCHPOINTS FOR HURTING PEOPLE
God's Answers for Your Daily Needs

Other TouchPoints Products:

TouchPoint Bible
TouchPoints
TouchPoints for Women
TouchPoints for Men
TouchPoints for Students
Touchpoints for Couples
TouchPoints for Leaders
TouchPoint Bible Promises
TouchPoints of Hope
TouchPoints for Troubled Times

TouchPoints
for Hurting People

GOD'S ANSWERS FOR

YOUR DAILY NEEDS

Tyndale House Publishers, Inc.
Wheaton, Illinois

General editors: Ronald A. Beers and V. Gilbert Beers

Managing editor: Rhonda K. O'Brien

Contributing writers: V. Gilbert Beers, Ronald A. Beers, Brian R. Coffey, Jonathan D. Gray, Shawn A. Harrison, Sanford D. Hull, Douglas J. Rumford.

Designed by Beth Sparkman

Edited by Linda K. Taylor

ISBN 0-8423-4228-1

Printed in the United States of America

09 08 07 06 05 04
 8   7   6   5   4   3   2   1

Dearest friend,

Whoever or whatever has hurt you, God loves you and longs to comfort you in your pain. It is my prayer that the pages that follow will point you to him.

Romans 8:35-39 *Can anything ever separate us from Christ's love? Does it mean he no longer loves us if we have trouble or calamity, or are persecuted, or are hungry or cold or in danger or threatened with death? . . . No, despite all these things, overwhelming victory is ours through Christ, who loved us. And I am convinced that nothing can ever separate us from his love. Death can't, and life can't. The angels can't, and the demons can't. Our fears for today, our worries about tomorrow, and even the powers of hell can't keep God's love away. Whether we are high above the sky or in the deepest ocean, nothing in all creation will ever be able to separate us from the love of God that is revealed in Christ Jesus our Lord.*

2 Corinthians 1:3 *All praise to the God and Father of our Lord Jesus Christ. He is the source of every mercy and the God who comforts us.*

—RHONDA K. O'BRIEN

This book is dedicated to my mother, Alice Bryant, who pointed me to Jesus. She met him face-to-face this year—at home at last, where there is no more hurt.

PREFACE

Psalm 119:111, 162   *Your decrees are my treasure; they are truly my heart's delight. . . . I rejoice in your word like one who finds a great treasure.*

Psalm 119:91, 160   *Your laws remain true today, for everything serves your plans. . . . All your words are true; all your just laws will stand forever.*

Psalm 119:105   *Your word is a lamp for my feet and a light for my path.*

What a treasure we have in God's Word! The Holy Bible is relevant to today's issues and gives solid guidance for daily living.

In this book you will find more than 100 topics that deal with hurts in our lives and how to overcome them and what the Bible says about each one. Each topic is listed alphabetically, with several questions, Scripture passages, and comments addressing each topic. In the index at the back of this book, you will find a complete listing of all the topics for quick reference. You can read through this book page by page or use it as a reference guide for topics of particular interest to you.

Although we could not cover all topics, questions, and Scriptures related to the subject of this book, our prayer is that you will continue to deliberately search God's Word. May you find God's answers as he longs to be your daily Guide. Enjoy your treasure hunt!

—THE EDITORS

2 Timothy 3:16-17 *All Scripture is inspired by God and is useful to teach us what is true and to make us realize what is wrong in our lives. It straightens us out and teaches us to do what is right. It is God's way of preparing us in every way, fully equipped for every good thing God wants us to do.*

Abandonment

(*see also* Loneliness, Neglect)

Does my suffering mean that God has abandoned me?

1 Peter 5:10 *After you have suffered a little while, he will restore, support, and strengthen you, and he will place you on a firm foundation.*
Rather than abandoning us when we suffer, God moves in to help us and comfort us with his presence. You may feel alone in your suffering, but God has compassion on you and promises an eternal reward waiting for you.

Will God abandon me during my difficult times?

Psalm 27:10 *Even if my father and mother abandon me, the Lord will hold me close.*

2 Corinthians 4:9 *We are hunted down, but God never abandons us. We get knocked down, but we get up again and keep going.*

1

Psalm 9:10 *Those who know your name trust in you, for you, O Lord, have never abandoned anyone who searches for you.*

Even if those on whom you most rely desert or neglect you during difficult times, God never will. In fact, your difficulties can become the means to experience God's presence even more intimately. When you face difficult times, you can trust that God has not abandoned you. Instead, he holds you close.

PROMISES FROM GOD

John 14:16 *I will ask the Father, and he will give you another Counselor, who will never leave you.*

Hebrews 13:5 *I will never fail you. I will never forsake you.*

Abortion

Did God really want me to be born? Does he have a plan for me?

Psalm 139:13-16 *You made all the delicate, inner parts of my body and knit me together in my mother's womb. Thank you for making me so wonderfully complex! Your workmanship is marvelous—and how well I know it. You watched me as I was being formed in utter seclusion, as I was woven together in the dark of the womb. You saw me before I was born.*

Every day of my life was recorded in your book. Every moment was laid out before a single day had passed. God not only knew all about you before you were born, he wanted you to be born and he has a plan for your life.

Don't I have the final say over what happens to my body?

1 Corinthians 6:12-13 *You may say, "I am allowed to do anything." But I reply, "Not everything is good for you." And even though "I am allowed to do anything," I must not become a slave to anything, . . . But our bodies were not made for sexual immorality. They were made for the Lord, and the Lord cares about our bodies.*

1 Corinthians 3:16-17 *Don't you realize that all of you together are the temple of God and that the Spirit of God lives in you? God will bring ruin upon anyone who ruins this temple. For God's temple is holy, and you Christians are that temple.* Your body is God's temple; his Spirit lives within you. Body, mind, and heart must do what is honoring and pleasing to him. Society says you have a choice; God says you should choose life.

Can God forgive me for having an abortion?

Psalm 51:3, 10, 12 *I recognize my shameful deeds—they haunt me day and night. . . . Create in me a clean heart, O God. . . . Restore to me again the joy of your salvation.*

3

Just as King David experienced the joy of total forgiveness after committing adultery and murder, so you can know God's forgiveness—for any sin—if you confess that sin to him.

Isaiah 1:18 No matter how deep the stain of your sins, I can remove it. I can make you as clean as freshly fallen snow. Even if you are stained as red as crimson, I can make you as white as wool.

1 John 1:9 But if we confess our sins to him, he is faithful and just to forgive us and to cleanse us from every wrong.

Ephesians 3:18 And may you have the power to understand, as all God's people should, how wide, how long, how high, and how deep his love really is. God can cleanse and heal you from any and all sin, no matter how big or terrible it might be. No sin is beyond God's forgiveness; no matter how great your sin, God's forgiveness is greater. No matter what you may have done in the past, let God restore you to wholeness through his amazing, boundless love for you.

PROMISE FROM GOD

Jeremiah 1:5 I knew you before I formed you in your mother's womb.

Abuse

(*see also* Anger, Used/Using Others/Feeling Used, Violence)

How do I heal the wounds of abuse?

Ephesians 4:31 *Get rid of all bitterness, rage, anger, harsh words, and slander, as well as all types of malicious behavior.*

Recognize that resentment, bitterness, and desire for revenge will only poison your own soul. Your hurt is real, but you must leave it with God. He will bring justice in his way and in his time.

Colossians 3:13 *Remember, the Lord forgave you, so you must forgive others.*

This is difficult, but important. If you refuse to forgive, you will only be hurting yourself. Forgiveness is the only way to purge your soul of the toxin of bitterness and a vengeful spirit. Remember that you did not deserve forgiveness for your sins, but Jesus forgave you by grace; likewise, an abuser does not deserve your forgiveness, but you can choose to forgive anyway. When you forgive, you are *not* saying the hurt isn't real, or that the event didn't matter, or that you will put yourself in a position where you might be harmed again. The person who hurt you doesn't need to be asked or told. The act of forgiveness can occur between you and God. All it means is that you

5

refuse to let the abuser have any more control in your life. Leave your hurt with God and allow him to comfort you and heal you.

Philippians 4:8 *Fix your thoughts on what is true and honorable and right. Think about things that are pure and lovely and admirable. Think about things that are excellent and worthy of praise.*
As you fill your mind with thoughts about God, there is less room to dwell on the past. Focus on the future and on all God's promises to you.

Is physical discipline of my child considered abuse?

Proverbs 29:15, 17 *To discipline and reprimand a child produces wisdom, but a mother is disgraced by an undisciplined child. . . . Discipline your children, and they will give you happiness and peace of mind.*

Proverbs 13:24 *If you refuse to discipline your children, it proves you don't love them; if you love your children, you will be prompt to discipline them.*
The Bible clearly advocates discipline of children, even physical discipline. But such disciplines must be done in love. Discipline that comes from unchecked anger can lead to abuse and violence, so we must be careful.

What is the best way to prevent abuse?

Romans 13:10 *Love does no wrong to anyone.*
Love restrains us from abusing a loved one—

physically or in any other way. This is not a roller-coaster love based on feelings, but a rock-solid commitment to protect and nurture regardless of the way we feel at a particular moment. Violence or abuse against a loved one is a warning signal that our love for that person is questionable. If you are concerned that you are sometimes abusive toward those you love, you should seek help to handle your anger. If you are in a situation where you are being abused, your best prevention is to talk to someone who can help you.

PROMISE FROM GOD
Psalm 34:18 *The Lord is close to the broken-hearted; he rescues those who are crushed in spirit.*

Addiction

(*see also* Temptation)

How can God break the power of addiction in my life?

Galatians 5:22-23 *When the Holy Spirit controls our lives, he will produce this kind of fruit in us: love, joy, peace, patience, kindness, goodness, faithfulness, gentleness, and self-control.*

Romans 8:5-8 *Those who are dominated by the sinful nature think about sinful things, but those who are controlled by the Holy Spirit think about things that please the Spirit. . . . That's why those who are still under the control of their sinful nature can never please God.*

God can break the power of addiction in your life when you give him control. He will come into your life and change your heart and your desires. Surrender to the Holy Spirit, and God will replace addictive drives with life-affirming desires.

Romans 6:16 *Don't you realize that whatever you choose to obey becomes your master? You can choose sin, which leads to death, or you can choose to obey God and receive his approval.*

Submission is a choice. Every day you stand at the crossroads, choosing sinful ways or God's way. The choice is yours.

Ephesians 5:18 *Don't be drunk with wine, because that will ruin your life. Instead, let the Holy Spirit fill and control you.*

It is imperative to admit your addiction and acknowledge its destructiveness. You must also recognize that you cannot overcome addiction without God's help.

Luke 1:37 *For nothing is impossible with God.*

In order to overcome your addiction, you must believe it is possible. You will have this confidence when you recognize the greatness of God's power at work in you and for you.

Ecclesiastes 4:9-10, 12 *Two people can accomplish more than . . . one; they get a better return for their labor. If one person falls, the other can reach out and help. But people who are alone when they fall are in real trouble. . . . A person standing alone can be attacked and defeated, but two can stand back-to-back and conquer. Three are even better, for a triple-braided cord is not easily broken.* It is almost impossible to overcome addiction by yourself. You need the consistent support of other people who love you, tell you the truth, and hold you accountable. Participating in some sort of addiction recovery support group is important, perhaps even essential, in order to overcome an addiction.

Romans 12:2 *Don't copy the behavior and customs of this world, but let God transform you into a new person by changing the way you think. Then you will know what God wants you to do, and you will know how good and pleasing his will really is.*

1 John 4:4 *You belong to God, my dear children. You have already won your fight, . . . because the Spirit who lives in you is greater than the spirit who lives in the world.*

1 John 5:4-5 *Every child of God defeats this evil world by trusting Christ to give the victory. And the ones who win this battle against the world are the ones who believe that Jesus is the Son of God.*

Freedom from addiction comes as you change your focus and your mind. You do this by trusting in Christ as your Savior and Lord and experiencing the power he brings into your life.

PROMISE FROM GOD
John 8:36 *So if the Son sets you free, you will indeed be free.*

Adultery

What is God's definition of adultery?

Hebrews 13:4 *Give honor to marriage, and remain faithful to one another in marriage. God will surely judge people who are immoral and those who commit adultery.*

Adultery is being unfaithful to one's spouse. Normally, this involves forming a sexual relationship with someone else, but even an intimate emotional relationship with another can become adulterous if it leads a person away from his or her spouse. Similarly, in the spiritual realm, we commit adultery against God when we are unfaithful to him by worshiping anything or anyone except him.

Mark 10:11 *He told them, "Whoever divorces his wife and marries someone else commits adultery against her."*

The commitment to remain faithful "until death do us part" is a serious commitment and should not be taken lightly. Breaking the marriage vow and joining with another is adultery.

Matthew 5:28 *Anyone who even looks at a woman with lust in his eye has already committed adultery with her in his heart.*
When we look at another with lust, we are being unfaithful to our spouse.

Why is it important for me not to get involved in adultery?

Proverbs 6:32 *But the man who commits adultery is an utter fool, for he destroys his own soul.*
Like most sin, adultery is a momentary act of pleasure that has dire consequences—a lifetime of regret and pain. The consequences of adultery are severe and lasting.

1 Corinthians 6:9-10 *Don't you know that those who do wrong will have no share in the Kingdom of God? . . . Those who indulge in sexual sin, who are . . . adulterers . . . none of these will have a share in the Kingdom of God.*
Even if we are not caught in our sin during our lifetime, we won't get away with it forever.

How do I protect myself from the hurt of getting into an adulterous relationship?

Proverbs 2:16 *Wisdom will save you from the immoral woman, from the flattery of the adulterous woman.*

God promises wisdom to those who ask him for it (see James 1:5). When you have wisdom, you will have the discernment to know how to avoid adultery. You still must make the choice to avoid adulterous relationships, but wisdom helps you recognize the early warning signs that you are moving in the wrong direction.

Proverbs 4:25-27 *Look straight ahead, and fix your eyes on what lies before you. Mark out a straight path for your feet; then stick to the path and stay safe. Don't get sidetracked; keep your feet from following evil.*

If looking can lead into adultery, then *not* looking will help you avoid it. It can be challenging to have "faithful eyes," but it is a key to your success in avoiding adultery.

Proverbs 5:3-9 *The lips of an immoral woman are as sweet as honey, and her mouth is smoother than oil. But the result is as bitter as poison, sharp as a double-edged sword. . . . So now, my sons, listen to me. Never stray from what I am about to say: Run from her! Don't go near the door of her house! If you do, you will lose your honor and hand over to merciless people everything you have achieved in life.*

When faced with temptation, you might be tempted to think that you can "handle it," but

12

the best course is to run away and not look back
(see Genesis 39:1-20).

Proverbs 5:15, 18 *Drink water from your
own well—share your love only with your wife. . . .
Let your wife be a fountain of blessing for you. Rejoice
in the wife of your youth.*
Adultery is more likely if you allow discontent-
ment to creep into your heart. Ask God to help
you be content and satisfied with your mate.
Then work on being the type of husband or wife
that your mate can be satisfied with as well!

PROMISE FROM GOD
Proverbs 6:24 *These commands and this teaching will keep you from the immoral woman, from the
smooth tongue of an adulterous woman.*

Anger

(*see also* Violence)

What are the effects of anger?

Genesis 27:41-43 *Esau hated Jacob because
he had stolen his blessing, and he said to himself, . . .
"I will kill Jacob." But someone got wind of what
Esau was planning and reported it to Rebekah. She
sent for Jacob and told him, ". . . Flee to your uncle
Laban in Haran."*
Anger isolates us from others.

Proverbs 22:24 *Keep away from angry, short-tempered people.*
Anger leads to conflict and arguments.

Psalm 37:8 *Stop your anger! . . . Do not envy others—it only leads to harm.*

James 1:20 *Your anger can never make things right in God's sight.*
Anger produces ungodliness and evil motives in us.

1 Samuel 20:30-31 *Saul boiled with rage at Jonathan. . . . "As long as that son of Jesse is alive, you'll never be king. Now go and get him so I can kill him!"*
Saul's jealous anger blinded him to the fact that God had already chosen David to be the next king because of his godly character. Saul's anger was so intense that he plotted to murder David. Anger blinds us to what is really good and right.

How should I deal with my own anger in relationships?

Ephesians 4:26 *And don't sin by letting anger gain control over you. Don't let the sun go down while you are still angry.*

Ephesians 4:31-32 *Get rid of all bitterness, rage, anger, harsh words, and slander, as well as all types of malicious behavior. Instead, be kind to each other, tenderhearted, forgiving one another, just as God through Christ has forgiven you.*

Proverbs 19:11 *People with good sense restrain their anger; they earn esteem by overlooking wrongs.* Anger must be dealt with quickly before it becomes bitterness, hatred, or revenge. As hard as it sounds, kindness and forgiveness melt anger away.

What is the best way to deal with an angry person?

Proverbs 29:8 *Mockers can get a whole town agitated, but those who are wise will calm anger.*

Proverbs 15:1 *A gentle answer turns away wrath, but harsh words stir up anger.*

Proverbs 22:24-25 *Keep away from angry, short-tempered people, or you will learn to be like them and endanger your soul.*

Reacting to anger with anger almost always intensifies the problem. Wisdom and gentleness almost always calm the angry person.

PROMISE FROM GOD

Psalm 103:8 *The Lord is merciful and gracious; he is slow to get angry and full of unfailing love.*

Apathy

What causes apathy?

Proverbs 29:7 *The godly know the rights of the poor; the wicked don't care to know.*

15

Ephesians 4:19 *They don't care anymore about right and wrong, and they have given themselves over to immoral ways. Their lives are filled with all kinds of impurity and greed.*

Sinful living causes apathy. Sin turns the spotlight on self and selfishness, so that care for others fades into darkness. When we focus only on ourselves, we become apathetic about anyone else's needs.

Deuteronomy 6:11-12 *The houses will be richly stocked with goods you did not produce. You will draw water from cisterns you did not dig, and you will eat from vineyards and olive trees you did not plant. When you have eaten your fill in this land, be careful not to forget the Lord, who rescued you from slavery in the land of Egypt.*

Nehemiah 9:28 *But when all was going well, your people turned to sin again, and once more you let their enemies conquer them.*

Success and complacency can lead to apathy. Preoccupation with material things leads to apathy because eventually we get tired of the things we have. The more we focus our affection on this world, the more apathetic we will become. The antidote for apathy is loving concern for others because godly relationships go on forever.

What can I do when I am feeling apathetic?

Isaiah 32:10 *In a short time—in just a little more than a year—you careless ones will suddenly begin to care. For your fruit crop will fail, and the harvest will never take place.*

Proverbs 20:13 *If you love sleep, you will end in poverty. Keep your eyes open, and there will be plenty to eat!*

Understand the negative consequences of apathy. This can help to motivate you to action.

Psalm 119:83 *I am shriveled like a wineskin in smoke, exhausted with waiting. But I cling to your principles and obey them.*

Obey God's commands even when you don't feel like it—in fact, even when you don't feel like doing anything. Such obedience keeps you close to God and prevents apathy from wreaking havoc in your life.

Proverbs 13:4 *Lazy people want much but get little, but those who work hard will prosper and be satisfied.*

Romans 12:11 *Never be lazy in your work, but serve the Lord enthusiastically.*

2 Thessalonians 3:11 *Yet we hear that some of you are living idle lives, refusing to work and wasting time meddling in other people's business.*

2 John 1:8 *Watch out, so that you do not lose the prize for which we have been working so hard. Be diligent so that you will receive your full reward.*

Revelation 3:19 *I am the one who corrects and disciplines everyone I love. Be diligent and turn from your indifference.*

Get to work! One of the best cures for apathy is diligent, enthusiastic, hard work! The more you do productive work for God, the more energy you have from seeing God's power working through you in miraculous ways.

What happens if apathy is allowed to grow in my life?

Revelation 3:15-16 *I know all the things you do, that you are neither hot nor cold. I wish you were one or the other! But since you are like luke-warm water, I will spit you out of my mouth!*

Hebrews 2:3 *What makes us think that we can escape if we are indifferent to this great salvation that was announced by the Lord Jesus himself? It was passed on to us by those who heard him speak.*

If you are feeling apathetic in your relationship with God, remember that it is only through him that you have purpose and eternal life. Ask God to renew your love for him.

Jeremiah 12:11 *They have made it an empty wasteland; I hear its mournful cry. The whole land is desolate, and no one even cares.*

Apathy often leads to destruction. Apathy is not a passive force that lulls you to sleep, but an aggressive force that tries to prevent you from doing anything meaningful for God.

Ezekiel 12:2 *Son of man, you live among rebels who could see the truth if they wanted to, but they don't want to. They could hear me if they would listen, but they won't listen because they are rebellious.*

Jeremiah 7:26 *But my people have not listened to me or even tried to hear. They have been stubborn and sinful—even worse than their ancestors.*

Apathy can also lead to a life of rebellion. If you don't care about life or what God wants to do in your life, why be concerned about what God thinks?

PROMISE FROM GOD
Ezekiel 11:19 *And I will give them singleness of heart and put a new spirit within them. I will take away their hearts of stone and give them tender hearts instead,*

Ashamed

What can cause people to feel ashamed?

Genesis 2:25; 3:7 *Now, although Adam and his wife were both naked, neither of them felt any shame. . . . At that moment, their eyes were opened, and they suddenly felt shame at their nakedness. So*

*they strung fig leaves together around their hips
to cover themselves.*

Ezra 9:6 *I prayed, "O my God, I am utterly
ashamed; I blush to lift up my face to you. For our
sins are piled higher than our heads, and our guilt
has reached to the heavens."*
Our sin can cause us to feel ashamed. If we think
about our sin, we can't help but be ashamed
of it. So instead of hiding it, we can ask God to
forgive us.

Ezra 8:22-23 *For I was ashamed to ask the king
for soldiers and horsemen to accompany us and protect
us from enemies along the way. After all, we had told
the king, "Our God protects all those who worship him,
but his fierce anger rages against those who abandon
him." So we fasted and earnestly prayed that our God
would take care of us, and he heard our prayer.*
We can feel ashamed and embarrassed when
what we say we believe does not correlate with
the way we live.

2 Samuel 10:4-5 *So Hanun seized David's
ambassadors and shaved off half of each man's beard,
cut off their robes at the buttocks, and sent them back
to David in shame. When David heard what had
happened, he sent messengers to tell the men to stay
at Jericho until their beards grew out, for they were
very embarrassed by their appearance.*
Being mistreated can cause us to feel ashamed.

How can my feelings of shame be used by God?

1 Peter 4:14, 19 *Be happy if you are insulted for being a Christian, for then the glorious Spirit of God will come upon you. . . . So if you are suffering according to God's will, keep on doing what is right, and trust yourself to the God who made you, for he will never fail you.*
The shame you suffer because of your relationship with Christ can become notes of joy when you recognize how he lovingly suffered for you.

2 Chronicles 30:15 *On the appointed day in midspring, . . . the people slaughtered their Passover lambs. Then the priests and Levites became ashamed, so they purified themselves and brought burnt offerings to the Temple of the Lord.*
Your shame should lead you to God, not away from God.

2 Thessalonians 3:14 *Take note of those who refuse to obey what we say in this letter. Stay away from them so they will be ashamed.*
Sometimes you must allow others to become ashamed of their sins so they have the possibility of being reconciled to God.

1 Corinthians 4:14 *I am not writing these things to shame you, but to warn you as my beloved children.*
Words of rebuke that lead to shame can also be

loving words of warning. Rebuke may not seem very loving, but it can be. If you have felt ashamed because of a rebuke, ask God to humble you enough to understand any truth in the rebuke and any change you should make as a result.

1 Corinthians 6:5 *I am saying this to shame you. Isn't there anyone in all the church who is wise enough to decide these arguments?*
Being ashamed can encourage you to take right action or make right decisions.

How can I avoid feeling ashamed?

Psalm 25:2-3 *I trust in you, my God! Do not let me be disgraced, or let my enemies rejoice in my defeat. No one who trusts in you will ever be disgraced, but disgrace comes to those who try to deceive others.*

Psalm 34:5 *Those who look to him for help will be radiant with joy; no shadow of shame will darken their faces.*

2 Timothy 1:12 *And that is why I am suffering here in prison. But I am not ashamed of it, for I know the one in whom I trust, and I am sure that he is able to guard what I have entrusted to him until the day of his return.*
Trust in God. The more you look to God, the more you get perspective on what brings shame as well as how to deal with needless feelings of shame.

Psalm 119:6 *Then I will not be disgraced when I compare my life with your commands.*

Psalm 119:78, 80 *Bring disgrace upon the arrogant people who lied about me; meanwhile, I will concentrate on your commandments. . . . May I be blameless in keeping your principles; then I will never have to be ashamed.*

Be obedient to God. Obedience helps you avoid sinful acts that lead to shame.

2 Timothy 2:15 *Work hard so God can approve you. Be a good worker, one who does not need to be ashamed and who correctly explains the word of truth.*

Be diligent. Hard work brings tangible accomplishments that will help you avoid needless shame.

1 John 2:28 *And now, dear children, continue to live in fellowship with Christ so that when he returns, you will be full of courage and not shrink back from him in shame.*

Let your daily life reflect your relationship with Christ. A strong fellowship with Christ leaves little place for needless shame.

Isaiah 49:23 *Kings and queens will serve you. They will care for all your needs. They will bow to the earth before you and lick the dust from your feet. Then you will know that I am the Lord. Those who wait for me will never be put to shame.*

Wait on the Lord. Lingering in the Lord's presence helps you bask in his glory. Your shame fades into the background.

PROMISE FROM GOD
Philippians 1:20 *For I live in eager expectation and hope that I will never do anything that causes me shame, but that I will always be bold for Christ, as I have been in the past, and that my life will always honor Christ, whether I live or I die.*

Betrayal

What should I do when I feel betrayed?
Psalm 55:20-22 *As for this friend of mine, he betrayed me; he broke his promises. His words are as smooth as cream, but in his heart is war. . . . Give your burdens to the Lord, and he will take care of you. He will not permit the godly to slip and fall.* Betrayal is like suddenly hitting a sheet of ice while driving. Your basis for trust is gone, and you go into a dangerous skid. But when you turn to the Lord, he throws sand on the road, restoring you to safety, helping you stop, think, and patiently seek his will in the difficult situation you face.

Jeremiah 12:6 *Even your own brothers, members of your own family, have turned on you.*

They have plotted, raising a cry against you. Do not trust them, no matter how pleasantly they speak.

Matthew 10:16 *Be as wary as snakes and as harmless as doves.*

When you realize you cannot trust a particular person, acting wisely includes taking steps to keep from getting hurt again. You can avoid revenge and grant forgiveness while still exercising prudent self-protection.

Genesis 50:19-21 *But Joseph told them, "Don't be afraid of me. Am I God, to judge and punish you? As far as I am concerned, God turned into good what you meant for evil. He brought me to the high position I have today so I could save the lives of many people. No, don't be afraid. Indeed, I myself will take care of you and your families." And he spoke very kindly to them, reassuring them.*

Recognize God's hand in your life. Even when someone sins against you, God can pick up the pieces and make something good from them.

Psalm 118:8 *It is better to trust the Lord than to put confidence in people.*

2 Timothy 2:13 *If we are unfaithful, he remains faithful, for he cannot deny himself.*

When others are unfaithful, you can take great comfort in God's unwavering faithfulness. Anchor your faith in the Lord, not in other frail human beings.

Where do I find the courage and strength to forgive my betrayer?

Romans 12:19-21 *Never avenge yourselves. Leave that to God. For it is written, "I will take vengeance; I will repay those who deserve it," says the Lord. Instead, do what the Scriptures say: "If your enemies are hungry, feed them. If they are thirsty, give them something to drink, and they will be ashamed of what they have done to you." Don't let evil get the best of you, but conquer evil by doing good.*

The worst response to betrayal is to give in to vengeance. The wisest response to betrayal is to stop the cycle of retaliation and begin the strategy of blessing. Trust God to judge your cause.

Matthew 6:12-14 *Forgive us our sins, just as we have forgiven those who have sinned against us. . . . If you forgive those who sin against you, your heavenly Father will forgive you.*

Forgiveness is the only road to freedom. A forgiven person forgives. Nothing that anyone has done against you compares with what you have done against God. Refusing to forgive another means you don't realize just how much God has forgiven you.

Promise from God

Romans 3:3 *True, some of them were unfaithful; but just because they broke their promises, does that mean God will break his promises?*

Bitterness

What is the result of unresolved bitterness?

Genesis 27:42 *She sent for Jacob and told him, "Esau is threatening to kill you."*

Job 5:2 *Surely resentment destroys the fool, and jealousy kills the simple.*

Proverbs 27:3 *A stone is heavy and sand is weighty, but the resentment caused by a fool is heavier than both.*

Unresolved bitterness leads to hatred, anger, jealousy, and revenge. It can keep you from fellowship with God and others and blinds you from noticing God's blessings.

How do I deal with bitterness toward others?

Mark 11:25 *But when you are praying, first forgive anyone you are holding a grudge against, so that your Father in heaven will forgive your sins, too.*

Acts 8:22-23 *Turn from your wickedness and pray to the Lord. Perhaps he will forgive your evil thoughts, for I can see that you are full of bitterness and held captive by sin.*

Ephesians 4:31-32 *Get rid of all bitterness, rage, anger, harsh words, and slander, as well as all types of malicious behavior. Instead, be kind to each other, tenderhearted, forgiving one another, just as God through Christ has forgiven you.*

Forgiveness lifts burdens, cancels debts, and frees you from chains of bitterness.

PROMISE FROM GOD
Hebrews 12:15 *Look after each other so that none of you will miss out on the special favor of God. Watch out that no bitter root of unbelief rises up among you, for whenever it springs up, many are corrupted by its poison.*

Brokenhearted

(*see also* Comfort, Encouragement, Grief, Suffering)

How can God use my broken heart to bring him glory?

Joel 2:13 *"Don't tear your clothing in your grief; instead, tear your hearts."* Return to the Lord your God, for he is gracious and merciful. He is not easily angered. He is filled with kindness and is eager not to punish you.

Your broken heart can lead you to God. Humility is a good starting place on the road to God because it puts God and your problems in proper perspective.

Psalm 51:17 *The sacrifice you want is a broken spirit. A broken and repentant heart, O God, you will not despise.*

2 Corinthians 7:9-10 *Now I am glad I sent it, not because it hurt you, but because the pain caused you to have remorse and change your ways. It was the kind of sorrow God wants his people to have, so you were not harmed by us in any way. For God can use sorrow in our lives to help us turn away from sin and seek salvation. We will never regret that kind of sorrow. But sorrow without repentance is the kind that results in death.*

Your broken heart can lead you to realization, confession, and repentance of sin. When your heart breaks, it sometimes reveals the sin within and the need for the Lord to wash that sin away.

Psalm 51:8-10 *Oh, give me back my joy again; you have broken me—now let me rejoice. Don't keep looking at my sins. Remove the stain of my guilt. Create in me a clean heart, O God. Renew a right spirit within me.*

Psalm 30:11 *You have turned my mourning into joyful dancing. You have taken away my clothes of mourning and clothed me with joy.*

Your brokenness leads to healing, and healing leads to rejoicing. When God does his healing in your life, you will rejoice and others will rejoice with you.

2 Corinthians 1:4, 6 *He comforts us in all our troubles so that we can comfort others. When others are troubled, we will be able to give them the*

same comfort God has given us. . . . So when we are weighed down with troubles, it is for your benefit and salvation! For when God comforts us, it is so that we, in turn, can be an encouragement to you. Then you can patiently endure the same things we suffer.
Your broken heart can help you comfort others. In your brokenness, you understand others who are broken.

How does God respond to the broken-hearted?

Psalm 34:18 *The Lord is close to the broken-hearted; he rescues those who are crushed in spirit.*

Psalm 147:3 *He heals the brokenhearted, binding up their wounds.*
The Lord comforts the brokenhearted by his presence, his compassion, his listening, his love, his healing, his encouragement, and his blessing.

What should I do when I am broken-hearted?

Psalm 130:1 *From the depths of despair, O Lord, I call for your help.*
Call to the Lord for his help. Be honest with your feelings. He who made you can heal your broken heart. He who loves you will draw you close.

Psalm 119:28, 50, 52, 92 *I weep with grief; encourage me by your word. . . . Your promise revives me; it comforts me in all my troubles. . . .*

I meditate on your age-old laws; O Lord, they comfort me. . . . If your law hadn't sustained me with joy, I would have died in my misery.

Look to the Word of God for help. Meditate on God's character, promises, and commitment to you. His word will comfort and encourage you.

Mark 14:34-36 *He told them, "My soul is crushed with grief to the point of death. Stay here and watch with me." He went on a little farther and fell face down on the ground. He prayed that, if it were possible, the awful hour awaiting him might pass him by. "Abba, Father," he said, "everything is possible for you. Please take this cup of suffering away from me. Yet I want your will, not mine."*

Look to God in honest prayer. Prayer puts you in touch with the source of all healing. He who created you for relationship longs to talk with you.

Ecclesiastes 3:4 *A time to cry and a time to laugh. A time to grieve and a time to dance.*

Acts 20:37 *They wept aloud as they embraced him in farewell.*

Express your emotions to trusted friends, your pastor, or a counselor. Sometimes God will provide comfort through the words and help of other believers.

PROMISES FROM GOD

Psalm 31:7   *I am overcome with joy because of your unfailing love, for you have seen my troubles, and you care about the anguish of my soul.*

2 Corinthians 1:3   *All praise to the God and Father of our Lord Jesus Christ. He is the source of every mercy and the God who comforts us.*

Childlessness

How does God show his compassion on the childless?

Psalm 139:13   *You made all the delicate, inner parts of my body and knit me together in my mother's womb.*
God not only pays attention to the activity of the womb, he is the God of the womb.

Judges 13:3   *The angel of the Lord appeared to Manoah's wife and said, "Even though you have been unable to have children, you will soon become pregnant and give birth to a son."*

Genesis 30:22   *Then God remembered Rachel's plight and answered her prayers by giving her a child.*
God has the ability to compassionately open the barren womb. Although we do not understand why he chooses to do this for some and not for

others, we can trust that he is a loving, attentive heavenly Father to us all.

Psalm 113:9 *He gives the barren woman a home, so that she becomes a happy mother. Praise the Lord!*
God gives special attention and compassion to the childless who long for children.

How can my spouse and I have an attitude of hope if we are childless?

Ruth 4:13 *So Boaz married Ruth and took her home to live with him. When he slept with her, the Lord enabled her to become pregnant, and she gave birth to a son.*

Job 10:10 *You guided my conception and formed me in the womb.*

Psalm 62:1, 5, 8 *I wait quietly before God, for my salvation comes from him. . . . I wait quietly before God, for my hope is in him. . . . O my people, trust in him at all times. Pour out your heart to him, for God is our refuge.*
Your hope and trust must be in God, the Creator of life, who can use any womb to create life. He wants you to honestly pour your heart out to him to seek what is best from him. He is a refuge for you in your time of pain, suffering, loss, and sorrow.

How can I help others who are childless?

Genesis 25:21 *Isaac pleaded with the Lord to give Rebekah a child because she was childless. So the Lord answered Isaac's prayer, and his wife became pregnant with twins.*
Pray to God on their behalf.

Proverbs 30:15-16 *There are three other things—no, four!—that are never satisfied: the grave, the barren womb, the thirsty desert, the blazing fire.*

1 Samuel 1:8 *"What's the matter, Hannah?" Elkanah would ask. "Why aren't you eating? Why be so sad just because you have no children? You have me—isn't that better than having ten sons?"*
Listen with understanding and without minimizing the hurt of childlessness. The greatest eloquence of sympathy is sometimes listening without saying anything.

Job 24:20-21 *Wicked people are broken like a tree in the storm. For they have taken advantage of the childless who have no protecting sons. They refuse to help the needy widows.*
Look for ways to be of practical assistance to families without children, especially as the husband and wife age.

PROMISE FROM GOD
Lamentations 3:25-26 *The Lord is wonderfully good to those who wait for him and seek him. So it is good to wait quietly for salvation from the Lord.*

Comfort

(*see also* Sympathy)

How does God comfort me?

Psalm 119:76 *Now let your unfailing love comfort me, just as you promised me, your servant.*
He loves you.

Romans 8:26 *And the Holy Spirit helps us in our distress. For we don't even know what we should pray for, nor how we should pray. But the Holy Spirit prays for us with groanings that cannot be expressed in words.*
He prays for you.

Psalm 10:17 *Lord, you know the hopes of the helpless. Surely you will listen to their cries and comfort them.*
He listens to you.

Psalm 147:3 *He heals the brokenhearted, binding up their wounds.*
He heals your broken heart.

2 Thessalonians 2:16-17 *May our Lord Jesus Christ and God our Father, who loved us and in his special favor gave us everlasting comfort and good hope, comfort your hearts and give you strength in every good thing you do and say.*
He gives you eternal hope.

How can the Bible give me comfort?

Psalm 119:49-50, 52, 54 *Remember your promise to me, for it is my only hope. Your promise revives me; it comforts me in all my troubles. . . . I meditate on your age-old laws; O Lord, they comfort me. . . . Your principles have been the music of my life throughout the years of my pilgrimage.*

Romans 15:4 *Such things were written in the Scriptures long ago to teach us. They give us hope and encouragement as we wait patiently for God's promises.* God's promises in the Bible can comfort and encourage you in this life and give you the confident assurance that you will one day live forever in peace and security with him.

PROMISE FROM GOD
Psalm 118:5 *In my distress I prayed to the Lord, and the Lord answered me and rescued me.*

Coping

How do I cope when life's pain becomes overwhelming?

Psalm 55:2 *Please listen and answer me, for I am overwhelmed by my troubles.*

Psalm 61:2 *From the ends of the earth, I will cry to you for help, for my heart is overwhelmed. Lead me to the towering rock of safety.*

When you are overwhelmed, go to God in prayer. When the whole world seems to ignore you, God listens.

Isaiah 43:2 *When you go through deep waters and great trouble, I will be with you. When you go through rivers of difficulty, you will not drown! When you walk through the fire of oppression, you will not be burned up; the flames will not consume you.*
When you are overwhelmed, God is there with power to help you. Alone, you will drown in deep waters of difficulty; with God, you will prevail.

Psalm 71:14 *But I will keep on hoping for you to help me; I will praise you more and more.*

Psalm 42:5-6 *Why am I discouraged? Why so sad? I will put my hope in God! I will praise him again—my Savior and my God!*
When you are overwhelmed, keep your hope in God's promises and keep praising him.

How do I cope when life's demands seem impossible?

Genesis 41:16 *"It is beyond my power to do this," Joseph replied. "But God will tell you what it means and will set you at ease."*

Matthew 19:26 *Jesus looked at them intently and said, "Humanly speaking, it is impossible. But with God everything is possible."*

Philippians 4:13 *For I can do everything with the help of Christ who gives me the strength I need.*
Remember: what seems impossible for you is never impossible for God.

Psalm 33:17 *Don't count on your warhorse to give you victory—for all its strength, it cannot save you.*

Psalm 44:6 *I do not trust my bow; I do not count on my sword to save me.*

Isaiah 31:1 *Destruction is certain for those who look to Egypt for help, trusting their cavalry and chariots instead of looking to the Lord, the Holy One of Israel.*

Proverbs 3:5 *Trust in the Lord with all your heart; do not depend on your own understanding.*

Psalm 39:7 *And so, Lord, where do I put my hope? My only hope is in you.*
Remember: your ultimate hope should not be in anyone or anything other than the Lord.

Ecclesiastes 2:11 *But as I looked at everything I had worked so hard to accomplish, it was all so meaningless. It was like chasing the wind. There was nothing really worthwhile anywhere.*

Colossians 3:23 *Work hard and cheerfully at whatever you do, as though you were working for the Lord rather than for people.*

Luke 10:40-42 *But Martha was worrying over the big dinner she was preparing. She came to Jesus* and said, "Lord, doesn't it seem unfair to you that my sister just sits here while I do all the work? Tell her to come and help me." But the Lord said to her, "My dear Martha, you are so upset over all these details! There is really only one thing worth being concerned about. Mary has discovered it—and I won't take it away from her."

Remember: you must confirm your activities, motives, and priorities with God and adjust them accordingly.

Exodus 18:18, 21-24 *"You're going to wear yourself out—and the people, too. This job is too heavy a burden for you to handle all by yourself. . . . Find some capable, honest men who fear God and hate bribes. Appoint them as judges. . . . They will help you carry the load, making the task easier for you. If you follow this advice, and if God directs you to do so, then you will be able to endure the pressures, and all these people will go home in peace." Moses listened to his father-in-law's advice and followed his suggestions.*

Remember: it is important to follow God's directions. Many times seeking godly advice may provide a workable solution you had not considered. God's wisdom may flow to you through godly counselors.

PROMISES FROM GOD

Psalm 145:14 *The Lord helps the fallen and lifts up those bent beneath their loads.*

Philippians 4:6-7 *Don't worry about anything; instead, pray about everything. Tell God what you need, and thank him for all he has done. If you do this, you will experience God's peace, which is far more wonderful than the human mind can understand. His peace will guard your hearts and minds as you live in Christ Jesus.*

Criticism

How should I respond to criticism? How do I evaluate whether it is constructive or destructive?

Proverbs 12:16-18 *A wise person stays calm when insulted. An honest witness tells the truth; a false witness tells lies. Some people make cutting remarks, but the words of the wise bring healing.*
Measure criticism according to the stature of the person who is giving it. Evaluate whether the criticism is coming from a person with a reputation for truth or lies. Ask yourself if the criticism is meant to help or hurt.

1 Corinthians 4:4 *My conscience is clear, but that isn't what matters. It is the Lord himself who will examine me and decide.*
Always work to maintain a clear conscience by being honest and trustworthy. This allows you to shrug off criticism you know is unjustified.

1 Peter 4:14 *Be happy if you are insulted for being a Christian, for then the glorious Spirit of God will come upon you.*

Consider it a privilege to be criticized for your faith in God. God has special blessings for those who patiently endure this kind of criticism.

Proverbs 15:31 *If you listen to constructive criticism, you will be at home among the wise.*

You shortchange your future when you reject truthful information about yourself. Sometimes it's painful to hear the truth, but it's worse to carry on without improvement.

PROMISE FROM GOD
Romans 14:18 *If you serve Christ with this attitude, you will please God. And other Christians will approve of you, too.*

Death

(*see also* Farewells, Loss, Sympathy)

Is death really the end?

John 11:25-26 *Jesus told her, "I am the resurrection and the life. Those who believe in me, even though they die like everyone else, will live again. They are given eternal life for believing in me and will never perish."*

1 Corinthians 15:54-55 *When this happens—when our perishable earthly bodies have been transformed into heavenly bodies that will never die—then at last the Scriptures will come true: "Death is swallowed up in victory. O death, where is your victory? O death, where is your sting?"*

Romans 8:10 *Since Christ lives within you, even though your body will die because of sin, your spirit is alive because you have been made right with God.* For those who trust in Christ, death is not the end, but only the beginning of an eternity of infinite joy with the Lord.

John 14:2 *There are many rooms in my Father's home, and I am going to prepare a place for you.* When we travel, it's comforting to know there's a place to stay at the end of the day. This same comfort is ours as we think of the end of this life. Though death is a great unknown, Jesus Christ has gone before us. He has prepared a glorious place for us to live forever.

How can I be certain that there is eternal life?

1 Corinthians 15:4-6, 20 *He was buried, and he was raised from the dead on the third day, as the Scriptures said. He was seen by Peter and then by the twelve apostles. After that, he was seen by more than five hundred of his followers at one time, most of whom are still alive, though some have died by*

now. . . . But the fact is that Christ has been raised from the dead. He has become the first of a great harvest of those who will be raised to life again.
The resurrection of Jesus is not mere religious myth or theory. The biblical record mentions eyewitnesses to the risen Jesus and encourages people to interview them. Historical investigation serves only to confirm the fact of the Resurrection. This, in turn, assures you of your eternal life.

Is fear of death or thinking about death a bad thing?

Psalm 90:12 *Teach us to make the most of our time, so that we may grow in wisdom.*

Colossians 3:1-2 *Since you have been raised to new life with Christ, set your sights on the realities of heaven. . . . Let heaven fill your thoughts.*
While fear of the unknown is natural, thoughts of death can be healthy if you are drawn to know more about God and make every day count for him. It is helpful to think of death as a beginning, not an end. It will be your entrance into eternal life with God.

Philippians 1:21 *For to me, living is for Christ, and dying is even better.*
Fear of dying may be an indication of a weak relationship with God or a lack of trust in God's promises. You must be ready to die (be at peace with yourself) in order to appreciate life fully.

Take time to ponder God's assurances of eternity and apply yourself to knowing and serving God. The more real God is to you, the less fearsome death will seem.

PROMISES FROM GOD

Psalm 49:15 *But as for me, God will redeem my life. He will snatch me from the power of death.*

Romans 6:23 *For the wages of sin is death, but the free gift of God is eternal life through Christ Jesus our Lord.*

Depression

What can I do when I'm depressed?

Psalm 42:5-6 *Why am I discouraged? Why so sad? I will put my hope in God! I will praise him again—my Savior and God! Now I am deeply discouraged, but I will remember your kindness.*

Depression is a time for soul-searching, for asking questions. We are often discouraged because we concentrate on our circumstances instead of on the Lord who will always care for us. The psalmist's questions awakened him to the reality that God alone is the source of comfort and hope. When you are depressed, remind yourself that God has been faithful to you in the past and will be faithful in the present and future, and then praise him for that.

Habakkuk 3:17-19 *Even though the fig trees have no blossoms, and there are no grapes on the vine; even though the olive crop fails, and the fields lie empty and barren; even though the flocks die in the fields, and the cattle barns are empty, yet I will rejoice in the Lord! I will be joyful in the God of my salvation. The Sovereign Lord is my strength! He will make me as surefooted as a deer and bring me safely over the mountains.*

Much depression is caused by trusting in the things of this world instead of in God. You will be disappointed if your happiness is based on security, prestige, possessions, and popularity. These things come and go. Trusting in God to lead you day by day helps you travel through the toughest times with surefooted confidence.

Psalm 92:1 *It is good to give thanks to the Lord, to sing praises to the Most High.*

Acts 16:22-25 *A mob quickly formed against Paul and Silas, and the city officials ordered them stripped and beaten with wooden rods. They were severely beaten, and then they were thrown into prison. . . . Around midnight, Paul and Silas were praying and singing hymns to God, and the other prisoners were listening.*

Praising the Lord will lift your mood. It is a deliberate act of obedience that is hard to do when you are down, but it produces immediate results. Praise the Lord for his unfailing, unconditional

love for you. Praise him for the gift of salvation
and eternal life. Praise him for anything good
you see around you. Praise him for his promise
to help you through your depression.

Psalm 143:7 *Come quickly, Lord, and answer
me, for my depression deepens. Don't turn away from
me, or I will die.*

Proverbs 16:20 *Those who listen to instruction
will prosper; those who trust the Lord will be happy.*
The Lord's strong presence in your life is the best
cure for depression. But with the Lord's help, you
may also need to seek the best medical or psycho-
logical help and ask him to use it to heal you.

Does feeling depressed mean something is wrong with my faith?

Judges 15:18 *Now Samson was very thirsty,
and he cried out to the Lord, "You have accomplished
this great victory. . . . Must I now die of thirst . . . ?"*

1 Kings 19:3-4 *Elijah was afraid and fled for
his life. . . . He sat down under a solitary broom tree
and prayed that he might die.*
Even for the people of God, depression can often
follow great achievement or spiritual victory. You
are on such a high that the only place to go is
down. If you recognize this, you will not be
surprised when you feel down soon after feeling
on top of the world. This is normal, but beware
of the common tendency to neglect God after a

spiritual victory. Instead, it is important at this time to fill your heart and mind with God's Word, which will encourage you about God's love and care and keep you from falling too low.

PROMISE FROM GOD
Psalm 40:2 *He lifted me out of the pit of despair.*

Dignity

(*see also* Insignificance, Self-Esteem, Worth/Worthiness)

What is dignity and where do we get it?

Genesis 1:27 *So God created people in his own image; God patterned them after himself; male and female he created them.*

Psalm 8:5 *For you made us only a little lower than God, and you crowned us with glory and honor.*

Isaiah 49:5 *And now the Lord speaks—he who formed me in my mother's womb to be his servant, who commissioned me to bring his people of Israel back to him. The Lord has honored me, and my God has given me strength.*

Psalm 149:4-5 *For the Lord delights in his people; he crowns the humble with salvation. Let the faithful rejoice in this honor.*

Psalm 62:7 *My salvation and my honor come from God alone. He is my refuge, a rock where no enemy can reach me.*

John 5:44 *No wonder you can't believe! For you gladly honor each other, but you don't care about the honor that comes from God alone.*

2 Thessalonians 1:12 *Then everyone will give honor to the name of our Lord Jesus because of you, and you will be honored along with him. This is all made possible because of the undeserved favor of our God and Lord, Jesus Christ.*

Dignity is understanding who God made us to be—human beings who bear his image. We have great worth and value and have been made for a special purpose. Lasting dignity comes from honoring our Creator.

PROMISES FROM GOD

Proverbs 22:1 *Choose a good reputation over great riches, for being held in high esteem is better than having silver or gold.*

Hebrews 13:18 *Pray for us, for our conscience is clear and we want to live honorably in everything we do.*

Disabilities

(*see also* Self-Esteem)

Does God care about disabled people?

Jeremiah 31:8 *For I will bring them from the north and from the distant corners of the earth. I will not forget the blind and lame, the expectant mothers about to give birth. A great company will return!*

God's compassionate purposes have always included the disabled. God loves every person equally, regardless of limitations.

Luke 7:22 *Then he told John's disciples, "Go back to John and tell him what you have seen and heard—the blind see, the lame walk, the lepers are cured, the deaf hear, the dead are raised to life, and the Good News is being preached to the poor."*

Throughout his earthly ministry, Jesus demonstrated special concern for those with disabilities. Jesus' concern for disabled people did not stay in his heart but reached out with help and healing.

Acts 3:7 *Then Peter took the lame man by the right hand and helped him up.*

As Christ's representatives, the apostles reached out to include and even heal the disabled. We must also reach out and help those in need.

Can God use disabled people?

Galatians 6:11 *Notice what large letters I use as I write these closing words in my own handwriting.*

The apostle Paul may have had a serious vision problem, yet the Lord was pleased to use him in mighty ways. We must never use our limitations as an excuse not to serve God.

Ruth 1:16 *But Ruth replied, "Don't ask me to leave you and turn back. I will go wherever you go and live wherever you live. Your people will be my people, and your God will be my God."*

Ruth had two significant disabilities—she was a foreigner and a widow—yet she is a model of loyalty and became an ancestor of the Messiah.

1 Corinthians 12:7 *A spiritual gift is given to each of us as a means of helping the entire church.*

God has given every Christian—including those with disabilities—a spiritual gift for serving others.

PROMISE FROM GOD

Ezekiel 34:15-16 *I myself will tend my sheep and cause them to lie down in peace, says the Sovereign Lord. . . . I will bind up the injured and strengthen the weak.*

Disappointment

How should I handle my disappointment with God?

Exodus 5:22 *So Moses went back to the Lord and protested.*

Go to God in prayer to try to understand his ways.

John 11:21 *Martha said to Jesus, "Lord, if you had been here, my brother would not have died."*

Be honest with God about your thoughts and feelings. He knows them anyway, so why try to hide them?

2 Corinthians 12:8-10 *Three different times I begged the Lord to take it away. Each time he said, "My gracious favor is all you need. My power works best in your weakness." So now I am glad to boast about my weaknesses, so that the power of Christ may work through me. . . . For when I am weak, then I am strong.*

You may not understand why God doesn't always take away your pain, but you can learn through disappointment that your weaknesses are great opportunities for God to work his power through you.

How should I deal with life's disappointments?

Psalm 63:1 *O God, you are my God; I earnestly search for you. My soul thirsts for you.*

51

In your disappointment, move toward God, not away from him. Running from the one who can help you is not wise.

Luke 5:4-5 *When he had finished speaking, he said to Simon, "Now go out where it is deeper and let down your nets, and you will catch many fish." "Master," Simon replied, "we worked hard all last night and didn't catch a thing. But if you say so, we'll try again."*
Listen to the Lord and trust him, even when it seems unreasonable.

Romans 8:28 *And we know that God causes everything to work together for the good of those who love God and are called according to his purpose for them.*
Accept God's ability to bring good still.

Is there a way to avoid or minimize disappointment?

Haggai 1:6, 9 *You have planted much but harvested little. . . . Why? Because my house lies in ruins, says the Lord Almighty, while you are all busy building your own fine houses.*
Put God first. Give him the first part of your money, the best minutes of your day, the highest priority in your life. By doing this you will learn to see what is truly important, and you will discover that there is nothing more rewarding

and satisfying than a relationship with the God who created you and loves you.

1 Peter 2:6 *As the Scriptures express it, "I am placing a stone in Jerusalem, a chosen cornerstone, and anyone who believes in him will never be disappointed."*
Put your faith, trust, and expectations in the Lord. Because he created you, you can learn only from him what he has planned for you.

Galatians 6:4 *Be sure to do what you should, for then you will enjoy the personal satisfaction of having done your work well, and you won't need to compare yourself to anyone else.*
Do what is right, and the satisfaction of a job well done will minimize disappointment.

PROMISE FROM GOD
Psalm 22:5 *You heard their cries for help and saved them. They put their trust in you and were never disappointed.*

Disillusionment

What can result from disillusionment?
Psalm 35:12 *They repay me with evil for the good I do. I am sick with despair.*
Despair.

Ecclesiastes 4:8 *This is the case of a man who is all alone, without a child or a brother, yet who works hard to gain as much wealth as he can. But then he asks himself, "Who am I working for? Why am I giving up so much pleasure now?" It is all so meaningless and depressing.*
Depression.

Isaiah 44:9 *How foolish are those who manufacture idols to be their gods. These highly valued objects are really worthless. They themselves are witnesses that this is so, for their idols neither see nor know. No wonder those who worship them are put to shame.*
Shame.

James 5:3 *Your gold and silver have become worthless. The very wealth you were counting on will eat away your flesh in hell. This treasure you have accumulated will stand as evidence against you on the day of judgment.*
Eternal judgment.

How can I recover from disillusionment?

Acts 14:15 *We have come to bring you the Good News that you should turn from these worthless things to the living God, who made heaven and earth, the sea, and everything in them.*
Ask God to help you turn from focusing on what is meaningless and turn to what is satisfying and fulfilling.

Hebrews 6:18-19 *So God has given us both his promise and his oath. These two things are unchangeable because it is impossible for God to lie. Therefore, we who have fled to him for refuge can take new courage, for we can hold on to his promise with confidence. This confidence is like a strong and trustworthy anchor for our souls. It leads us through the curtain of heaven into God's inner sanctuary.* Place your faith and hope confidently in God's character, God's Word, and God's presence.

How can I prevent disillusionment?

Deuteronomy 6:5 *And you must love the Lord your God with all your heart, all your soul, and all your strength.*

Proverbs 4:23 *Above all else, guard your heart, for it affects everything you do.*

1 Thessalonians 5:8 *But let us who live in the light think clearly, protected by the body armor of faith and love, and wearing as our helmet the confidence of our salvation.* Love God above anything else. Guard your affections and think clearly using faith, love, and the confidence of salvation as your protection.

Matthew 6:33 *He will give you all you need from day to day if you live for him and make the Kingdom of God your primary concern.*

Acts 20:24 *But my life is worth nothing unless I use it for doing the work assigned me by the Lord*

Jesus—the work of telling others the Good News about God's wonderful kindness and love.
Dedicate yourself to the priority of accomplishing God's mission on earth, not yours.

Ecclesiastes 11:8 *When people live to be very old, let them rejoice in every day of life. But let them also remember that the dark days will be many. Everything still to come is meaningless.*

Romans 8:28 *And we know that God causes everything to work together for the good of those who love God and are called according to his purpose for them.*

Hebrews 10:35 *Do not throw away this confident trust in the Lord, no matter what happens. Remember the great reward it brings you!*
Remember that God is sovereign and rewards those who trust in him.

PROMISES FROM GOD

Psalm 119:37 *Turn my eyes from worthless things, and give me life through your word.*

Proverbs 10:28 *The hopes of the godly result in happiness, but the expectations of the wicked are all in vain.*

Divorce

What does the Bible say about divorce?

Malachi 2:14-16 *You cry out, "Why has the Lord abandoned us?" I'll tell you why! Because the Lord witnessed the vows you and your wife made to each other on your wedding day. . . . But you have been disloyal. . . . Didn't the Lord make you one . . .? In body and spirit you are his. . . . So guard yourself; remain loyal. . . . "For I hate divorce!" says the Lord.*
God sees divorce as wrong because it is the breaking of a binding commitment and it is tearing in half and destroying what God has made into one. A conscious decision to be unfaithful has been made by one or both spouses.

Matthew 19:3 *Some Pharisees came and tried to trap him. . . . "Should a man be allowed to divorce his wife for any reason?"*
There is a wide range of interpretation concerning this passage (Matthew 19:3-9), with wide application to specific situations. The Old Testament provided for specific rules concerning divorce and limited remarriage in special cases (Deuteronomy 24:1-4), while at the same time making it clear that divorce is not God's intention (Malachi 2:14-16). The New Testament also makes it clear that divorce is wrong (Matthew 5:31-32; 1 Corinthians 7:10-11), while allowing

for the limited exceptions Jesus mentions in
Matthew 19:3-9.

How can I ever forgive someone who has hurt me so deeply?

Colossians 3:13 *You must make allowance
for each other's faults and forgive the person who
offends you. Remember, the Lord forgave you, so
you must forgive others.*

Matthew 5:44 *But I say, love your enemies!
Pray for those who persecute you!*
If you are striving to be godly, you must do what
God would do, and he would forgive. This may
be the hardest thing you will ever have to do.
Forgiveness is not easy, but is necessary in order
to move on. It also demonstrates that love, not
bitterness or hatred, rules your heart.

How do I move forward as a single person?

1 Corinthians 7:7, 32-35 *God gives some
the gift of marriage, and to others he gives the gift of
singleness. . . . In everything you do, I want you to be
free from the concerns of this life. An unmarried man
can spend his time doing the Lord's work and thinking
how to please him. But a married man can't do that so
well. He has to think about his earthly responsibilities
and how to please his wife. His interests are divided.
In the same way, a woman who is no longer married
or has never been married can be more devoted to the*

Lord in body and in spirit, while the married woman must be concerned about her earthly responsibilities and how to please her husband. I am saying this for your benefit, not to place restrictions on you.
Make the most of your singleness by wholeheartedly serving the Lord. It will be through your service that you find what God most wants for you—whether to be single or married.

PROMISES FROM GOD
Ephesians 3:18   *May you have the power to understand . . . how wide, how long, how high, and how deep his love really is.*

Matthew 19:6   *Since they are no longer two but one, let no one separate them, for God has joined them together.*

Drinking/Drunkenness

When does drinking become wrong?
Ephesians 5:18   *Don't be drunk with wine, because that will ruin your life. Instead, let the Holy Spirit fill and control you.*

Exodus 32:6   *So the people got up early the next morning to sacrifice burnt offerings and peace offerings. After this, they celebrated with feasting and drinking, and indulged themselves in pagan revelry.*

Proverbs 23:29-32 *Who has anguish? Who has sorrow? Who is always fighting? Who is always complaining? Who has unnecessary bruises? Who has bloodshot eyes? It is the one who spends long hours in the taverns, trying out new drinks. Don't let the sparkle and smooth taste of wine deceive you. For in the end it bites like a poisonous serpent; it stings like a viper.* Drinking becomes wrong when it leads to drunkenness, when it influences your actions, or when it causes you to disobey and dishonor God. (For minors, this includes drinking at any time.)

I'm addicted to drinking. Can God help me?

1 Corinthians 10:13 *Remember that the temptations that come into your life are no different from what others experience. And God is faithful. He will keep the temptation from becoming so strong that you can't stand up against it. When you are tempted, he will show you a way out so that you will not give in to it.*

God can and will help anyone who is trapped by an addiction if that person will confess the sin, call upon him to help, and obediently follow his way.

PROMISE FROM GOD

2 Corinthians 5:17 *What this means is that those who become Christians become new persons. They are not the same anymore, for the old life is gone. A new life has begun!*

Drugs

What does the Bible say about drugs?

1 Corinthians 6:12-13 *You may say, "I am allowed to do anything." But I reply, "Not everything is good for you." And even though "I am allowed to do anything," I must not become a slave to anything. . . . Our bodies . . . were made for the Lord, and the Lord cares about our bodies.*

1 Corinthians 6:19-20 *Or don't you know that your body is the temple of the Holy Spirit, who lives in you and was given to you by God? You do not belong to yourself, for God bought you with a high price. So you must honor God with your body.*

1 Corinthians 10:31 *Whatever you eat or drink or whatever you do, you must do all for the glory of God.*

The Bible doesn't talk about drugs as we know of them today, but it does talk very specifically about not putting things into our bodies that are harmful or that are not glorifying to God. Taking drugs is trying to get a "high"—a feeling of ecstasy and satisfaction that is a cheap substitute for allowing the Holy Spirit to control our lives.

We are told that everything in moderation is OK. Can't that apply to drugs, too?

2 Peter 2:19 *They promise freedom, but they*

61

themselves are slaves to sin and corruption. For you are a slave to whatever controls you.

Whatever has control over you is your master. If God is your master, he will raise you up and encourage you, but the master of drugs will only tear you down and make you a slave to its addictive power.

PROMISE FROM GOD

Romans 8:5 *Those who are dominated by the sinful nature think about sinful things, but those who are controlled by the Holy Spirit think about things that please the Spirit.*

Empathy

How is God empathetic toward me?

Romans 5:6, 8 *When we were utterly helpless, Christ came at just the right time and died for us sinners. . . . But God showed his great love for us by sending Christ to die for us while we were still sinners.*

Isaiah 63:9 *In all their suffering he also suffered, and he personally rescued them. In his love and mercy he redeemed them. He lifted them up and carried them through all the years.*

Hebrews 4:15 *This High Priest of ours under-stands our weaknesses, for he faced all of the same temptations we do, yet he did not sin.*

Romans 8:34 *Who then will condemn us? Will Christ Jesus? No, for he is the one who died for us and was raised to life for us and is sitting at the place of highest honor next to God, pleading for us.*

Romans 8:26-27 *And the Holy Spirit helps us in our distress. For we don't even know what we should pray for, nor how we should pray. But the Holy Spirit prays for us with groanings that cannot be expressed in words. And the Father who knows all hearts knows what the Spirit is saying, for the Spirit pleads for us believers in harmony with God's own will.* God the Father loves us and planned to rescue us from the pain and eternal consequences of sin, which Jesus successfully accomplished through his life, death, and resurrection. Because Jesus came to earth as a human being, he can empa-thize with us. He understands our weaknesses and our fears. Both Jesus and the Holy Spirit plead for you today that you would be free from the hurt which comes from sin and experience the joy and freedom of a relationship with the eternal God.

How can I be more empathetic?

Galatians 6:2 *Share each other's troubles and problems, and in this way obey the law of Christ.*

Hebrews 13:3 *Don't forget about those in prison. Suffer with them as though you were there yourself. Share the sorrow of those being mistreated, as though you feel their pain in your own bodies.*

1 Corinthians 12:26 *If one part suffers, all the parts suffer with it, and if one part is honored, all the parts are glad.*

Romans 12:15 *When others are happy, be happy with them. If they are sad, share their sorrow.* You should be more than merely concerned about others' troubles and problems. To be empathetic, you need to be emotionally involved in other people's lives, sharing their troubles and problems.

Luke 10:36-37 *"Now which of these three would you say was a neighbor to the man who was attacked by bandits?" Jesus asked. The man replied, "The one who showed him mercy." Then Jesus said, "Yes, now go and do the same."*
We can show more empathy by helping a person in need.

Luke 6:31 *Do for others as you would like them to do for you.*
You can minister in ways you would like to be ministered to in similar circumstances. When you don't know what to do, ask what you would want someone to do for you in that situation.

PROMISE FROM GOD

2 Corinthians 1:3-4 *All praise to the God and Father of our Lord Jesus Christ. He is the source of every mercy and the God who comforts us. He comforts us in all our troubles so that we can comfort others.*

Emptiness

How do I fill the emptiness inside of me?

Revelation 4:11 *You are worthy, O Lord our God, to receive glory and honor and power. For you created everything, and it is for your pleasure that they exist and were created.*

Only God can fill the emptiness inside of you because he created you with a longing for him. When you invite him into your life, you will find true satisfaction and fulfillment.

1 Peter 1:18 *For you know that God paid a ransom to save you from the empty life you inherited from your ancestors. And the ransom he paid was not mere gold or silver.*

Titus 3:5-6 *He saved us, not because of the good things we did, but because of his mercy. He washed away our sins and gave us a new life through the Holy Spirit. He generously poured out the Spirit upon us because of what Jesus Christ our Savior did.*

When you accept God's gift of salvation and believe in Jesus Christ as Savior, you are filled with his Holy Spirit. The presence of God goes with you, along with his love, his help, his encouragement, his peace, and his comfort.

Colossians 2:10 *You are complete through your union with Christ. He is the Lord over every ruler and authority in the universe.*

John 1:16 *We have all benefited from the rich blessings he brought to us—one gracious blessing after another.*

John 4:13-14 *Jesus replied, "People soon become thirsty again after drinking this water. But the water I give them takes away thirst altogether. It becomes a perpetual spring within them, giving them eternal life."* You experience life to the fullest when you are engaged in a relationship with Jesus Christ, who gives you blessings here on earth and the promise of eternal life with him.

Where can I find real meaning and purpose in life?

Ephesians 4:13 *Until we come to such unity in our faith and knowledge of God's Son that we will be mature and full grown in the Lord, measuring up to the full stature of Christ.*

1 Peter 2:2 *You must crave pure spiritual milk so that you can grow into the fullness of your salvation. Cry out for this nourishment as a baby cries for milk.*

You find meaning and purpose in life as you grow in your relationship with Jesus, for he alone offers eternal life in heaven.

2 Timothy 2:21   *If you keep yourself pure, you will be a utensil God can use for his purpose. Your life will be clean, and you will be ready for the Master to use you for every good work.*

Psalm 57:2   *I cry out to God Most High, to God who will fulfill his purpose for me.*

1 Corinthians 15:58   *So, my dear brothers and sisters, be strong and steady, always enthusiastic about the Lord's work, for you know that nothing you do for the Lord is ever useless.*

You find meaning and purpose in life as you are used by God for his purposes.

PROMISE FROM GOD
John 10:10   *The thief's purpose is to steal and kill and destroy. My purpose is to give life in all its fullness.*

Encouragement

(*see also* Brokenhearted, Grief)

How does God encourage me?

Matthew 9:2   *Some people brought to him a paralyzed man on a mat. Seeing their faith, Jesus*

said to the paralyzed man, "Take heart, son! Your sins are forgiven."
He forgives your sins.

1 Kings 19:4-6 *Then he went on alone into the desert, traveling all day. He sat down under a solitary broom tree and prayed that he might die. "I have had enough, Lord," he said. . . . But as he was sleeping, an angel touched him and told him, "Get up and eat!" He looked around and saw some bread baked on hot stones and a jar of water!*
He meets your needs at just the right time.

Psalm 138:3 *When I pray, you answer me; you encourage me by giving me the strength I need.*
He gives you strength when you ask.

Psalm 119:25, 28 *I lie in the dust, completely discouraged; revive me by your word. . . . I weep with grief; encourage me by your word.*

Romans 15:4 *Such things were written in the Scriptures long ago to teach us. They give us hope and encouragement as we wait patiently for God's promises.*
He's given his written Word to revive you and offer you hope.

Hebrews 12:5 *Have you entirely forgotten the encouraging words God spoke to you, his children? He said, "My child, don't ignore it when the Lord disciplines you, and don't be discouraged when he corrects you."*

Even his discipline is an encouragement, for you know it is for your ultimate good.

How can I handle discouragement?

2 Chronicles 20:15 *Don't be discouraged by this mighty army, for the battle is not yours, but God's.*

Looking at circumstances instead of focusing on God can bring discouragement. It would have been easy for the people of Judah to see only the vast enemy army and not God standing by to destroy it. Stay focused on God.

1 Peter 5:8-9 *Be careful! Watch out for the attacks from the Devil, your great enemy. He prowls around like a roaring lion, looking for some victim to devour. Take a firm stand against him, and be strong in your faith. Remember that your Christian brothers and sisters all over the world are going through the same kind of suffering you are.*

Suffering produces discouragement, which causes vulnerability to Satan's attacks. Stay close to God's Word and other believers during these difficult times.

Psalm 73:2-3 *But as for me, I came so close to the edge of the cliff! My feet were slipping, and I was almost gone. For I envied the proud when I saw them prosper despite their wickedness.*

Stop focusing on the success of others and start looking at all God has given you.

PROMISE FROM GOD
2 Thessalonians 2:16-17 *May our Lord Jesus Christ and God our Father . . . comfort your hearts and give you strength in every good thing you do and say.*

Endurance

(*see also* Perseverance, Persistence)

Why should I keep on trying when I feel like quitting?

1 Timothy 6:11 *But you, Timothy, belong to God; so run from all these evil things, and follow what is right and good. Pursue a godly life, along with faith, love, perseverance, and gentleness.*

1 Peter 2:20 *Of course, you get no credit for being patient if you are beaten for doing wrong. But if you suffer for doing right and are patient beneath the blows, God is pleased with you.*

Revelation 13:10 *The people who are destined for prison will be arrested and taken away. Those who are destined for death will be killed. But do not be dismayed, for here is your opportunity to have endurance and faith.*

Endurance is commanded and commended by God. It is necessary to reaching the goal of a life well lived and, ultimately, of eternal life.

70

Luke 9:62 *But Jesus told him, "Anyone who puts a hand to the plow and then looks back is not fit for the Kingdom of God."*

Mark 13:13 *And everyone will hate you because of your allegiance to me. But those who endure to the end will be saved.*

Hebrews 3:6 *But Christ, the faithful Son, was in charge of the entire household. And we are God's household, if we keep up our courage and remain confident in our hope in Christ.*

Endurance is the sign that your faith is for real because it shows that you have eternal goals clearly in mind.

How do I develop endurance?

Colossians 1:10-11 *Then the way you live will always honor and please the Lord, and you will continually do good, kind things for others. All the while, you will learn to know God better and better. We also pray that you will be strengthened with his glorious power so that you will have all the patience and endurance you need. May you be filled with joy.*

2 Thessalonians 3:5 *May the Lord bring you into an ever deeper understanding of the love of God and the endurance that comes from Christ.*

Ephesians 6:13 *Use every piece of God's armor to resist the enemy in the time of evil, so that after the battle you will still be standing firm.*

Endurance originates with God. He is your source of the power and perseverance you need to endure.

Hebrews 12:2-3 *We do this by keeping our eyes on Jesus, on whom our faith depends from start to finish. He was willing to die a shameful death on the cross because of the joy he knew would be his afterward. Now he is seated in the place of highest honor beside God's throne in heaven. Think about all he endured when sinful people did such terrible things to him, so that you don't become weary and give up.* You have the example of Jesus on which to focus as your model for endurance. The next time you are tempted to give up, think of Jesus on the cross.

Hebrews 12:1 *Therefore, since we are surrounded by such a huge crowd of witnesses to the life of faith, let us strip off every weight that slows us down, especially the sin that so easily hinders our progress. And let us run with endurance the race that God has set before us.*
Get rid of sin, for it drags you down and keeps you from enduring.

Romans 5:3 *We can rejoice, too, when we run into problems and trials, for we know that they are good for us—they help us learn to endure.*

James 1:2-4 *Dear brothers and sisters, whenever trouble comes your way, let it be an opportunity for* joy. For when your faith is tested, your endurance has a chance to grow. So let it grow, for when your endurance is fully developed, you will be strong in character and ready for anything.

Of course, you don't like problems, trials, troubles, and the testing of your faith, for they can drag you down. But they can also lift you up, and when they do, you have learned endurance. With God's strength, you can learn to endure despite these things. Without God's strength you falter because of these things.

PROMISES FROM GOD

Hebrews 3:14 *For if we are faithful to the end, trusting God just as firmly as when we first believed, we will share in all that belongs to Christ.*

Hebrews 10:36 *Patient endurance is what you need now, so you will continue to do God's will. Then you will receive all that he has promised.*

Enemies

(*see also* Spiritual Warfare, Victory, War)

How should I respond to my enemies?

Luke 6:27-29 *But if you are willing to listen, I say, love your enemies. Do good to those who hate you. Pray for the happiness of those who curse you. Pray for those who hurt you. If someone slaps you on* one cheek, turn the other cheek. If someone demands your coat, offer your shirt also.

Romans 12:20-21 *Instead, do what the Scriptures say: "If your enemies are hungry, feed them. If they are thirsty, give them something to drink, and they will be ashamed of what they have done to you." Don't let evil get the best of you, but conquer evil by doing good.*

Luke 23:34 *Jesus said, "Father, forgive these people, because they don't know what they are doing." And the soldiers gambled for his clothes by throwing dice.*

1 Peter 3:9 *Don't repay evil for evil. Don't retaliate when people say unkind things about you. Instead, pay them back with a blessing. That is what God wants you to do, and he will bless you for it.*

Proverbs 24:17-18 *Do not rejoice when your enemies fall into trouble. Don't be happy when they stumble. For the Lord will be displeased with you and will turn his anger away from them.*

Romans 12:19 *Dear friends, never avenge yourselves. Leave that to God. For it is written, "I will take vengeance; I will repay those who deserve it," says the Lord.*

Respond to your enemies—no matter what they try to do—with loving forgiveness. Your actions toward your enemies should include prayer for them as well as acts of kindness. Your words should be gentle. Your attitude should not be one of revenge or ill will. This is what Jesus would do. And this is what sets you apart from the rest of the world. When you act this way, the world will take notice.

PROMISES FROM GOD

Leviticus 19:18 *Never seek revenge or bear a grudge against anyone, but love your neighbor as yourself. I am the Lord.*

Matthew 10:28-31 *Don't be afraid of those who want to kill you. They can only kill your body; they cannot touch your soul. Fear only God, who can destroy both soul and body in hell. Not even a sparrow, worth only half a penny, can fall to the ground without your Father knowing it. And the very hairs on your head are all numbered. So don't be afraid; you are more valuable to him than a whole flock of sparrows.*

Failure

(*see also* Mistakes)

Does failure make God love me less?

Hebrews 2:17-18 *Therefore, it was necessary for Jesus to be in every respect like us, his brothers and sisters, so that he could be our merciful and faithful High Priest before God. He then could offer a sacrifice that would take away the sins of the people. Since*

*he himself has gone through suffering and temptation,
he is able to help us when we are being tempted.*

Hebrews 4:15-16 *This High Priest of ours
understands our weaknesses. . . . So let us come boldly
to the throne of our gracious God . . . [to] find grace
to help us when we need it.*

God loves us unconditionally. Jesus Christ, our
High Priest, entered fully into human experience
and knows our trials and temptations. While
caring parents may be hurt or saddened by a
child's failure, that failure doesn't make them
love the child less. In fact, failure often awakens
greater tenderness and support toward the child.
In the same way, the Lord understands your
weaknesses and failures and loves you in spite
of them.

When I have failed, how do I get past it and move on?

1 Kings 8:33-34 *If your people Israel are
defeated by their enemies because they have sinned
against you, and if they turn to you and call on your
name and pray to you here in this Temple, then hear
from heaven and forgive their sins and return them
to this land you gave their ancestors.*

Turning to God in repentance and trust is the best
response you can have to failure.

1 John 2:1-2 *My dear children, I am writing
this to you so that you will not sin. But if you do sin,*

there is someone to plead for you before the Father. He is Jesus Christ, the one who pleases God completely. He is the sacrifice for our sins. He takes away not only our sins but the sins of all the world.

God gave his Son, Jesus Christ, to pay the debt of our failure and bring us back into full fellowship with him. The wonder of the gospel is that our failure revealed God's greatest success. Remembering what Christ did for you can help you to move on past the failure.

Proverbs 24:16 *They may trip seven times, but each time they will rise again. But one calamity is enough to lay the wicked low.*

Micah 7:8 *Though I fall, I will rise again. Though I sit in darkness, the Lord himself will be my light.*

2 Corinthians 4:9 *We are hunted down, but God never abandons us. We get knocked down, but we get up again and keep going.*

The best response to failure is to get up again, holding on to the hope that God gives you through faith.

1 Corinthians 10:6-7 *These events happened as a warning to us, so that we would not crave evil things as they did or worship idols as some of them did.*

Remember that failure can be helpful; it can teach you important lessons about what to avoid in the future. You need not repeat your mistakes or the mistakes you recognize in others!

Lamentations 3:23 *Great is his faithfulness; his mercies begin afresh each day.*
We all long for a clean start, a new slate, a chance to begin again. That's why many people get excited about New Year's resolutions. But every day is a new start in God's mercy. By God's grace and love you are freed from the burden of sin and failure so that you can start fresh.

Hebrews 12:10-11 *For our earthly fathers disciplined us for a few years, doing the best they knew how. But God's discipline is always right and good for us because it means we will share in his holiness. No discipline is enjoyable while it is happening—it is painful! But afterward there will be a quiet harvest of right living for those who are trained in this way.*
Failure doesn't determine your identity or your worth; it is simply feedback on how you are doing. Because God has adopted us as his children, he uses failures to train us, to reveal his love, and to shape us in holiness. Failure is not a dead end. In Christ it becomes the doorway to lasting change.

PROMISES FROM GOD

Psalm 37:23-24 *The steps of the godly are directed by the Lord. He delights in every detail of their lives. Though they stumble, they will not fall, for the Lord holds them by the hand.*

Farewells

(*see also* Death)

What will help me say good-bye in a healthy and positive way?

Acts 20:36-38 *When he had finished speaking, he knelt and prayed with them. They wept aloud as they embraced him in farewell, sad most of all because he had said that they would never see him again.*
Praying together and being open and honest about the pain of parting are important to healthy good-byes.

Philemon 1:7 *I myself have gained much joy and comfort from your love, my brother, because your kindness has so often refreshed the hearts of God's people.*
Before parting, thank people for what they have meant to you.

Genesis 12:4 *So Abram departed, as the Lord had instructed him.*
Seeing God's hand in your circumstances and following God's call in your life will give you greater security as you say good-bye, even though parting will still not be easy.

Psalm 139:9-10 *If I ride the wings of the morning, if I dwell by the farthest oceans, even there*

*your hand will guide me, and your strength will
support me.*

Never stop reminding yourself that God is the
constant in your life. You will never say good-bye
to him, or he to you. No matter where you have
to go, even across the "farthest oceans," even
there God's hand will guide you and give you
strength for the task ahead.

Acts 20:32 *And now I entrust you to God and
the word of his grace—his message that is able to
build you up and give you an inheritance with all
those he has set apart for himself.*

There is great comfort in knowing that God will
take care of those to whom you say farewell. God
is near to those with whom you are far apart.

2 Timothy 4:7 *I have fought a good fight, I
have finished the race, and I have remained faithful.*
Parting is easier if you have lived in such a way
as to minimize regrets and unfinished business.
Live each day with others as if you must say
good-bye tomorrow.

2 Timothy 1:4 *I long to see you again, for I
remember your tears as we parted. And I will be filled
with joy when we are together again.*
Anticipate the next meeting.

PROMISES FROM GOD
Matthew 28:20 *And be sure of this: I am with
you always, even to the end of the age.*

John 14:27-28 *I am leaving you with a gift—peace of mind and heart. . . . Remember what I told you: I am going away, but I will come back to you again.*

Financial Difficulties

(*see also* Poor/Poverty)

What are some of God's principles for financial health?

Proverbs 13:11 *Wealth from get-rich-quick schemes quickly disappears; wealth from hard work grows.*

Trying to get rich quickly usually backfires. Dedicate yourself to hard work over time. If something seems too good to be true, it probably is.

Proverbs 21:17 *Those who love pleasure become poor; wine and luxury are not the way to riches.*

Living a lifestyle beyond your means will lead to financial distress. Learning to say no and do without builds financial discipline, which relieves stress.

Proverbs 22:7 *Just as the rich rule the poor, so the borrower is servant to the lender.*

Undisciplined use of credit is a recipe for ruin.

Proverbs 6:10-11 *A little extra sleep, a little more slumber, a little folding of the hands to rest— and poverty will pounce on you like a bandit; scarcity will attack you like an armed robber.*
Initiative, energy, and self-discipline are essential for financial health. Laziness doesn't put money in the bank.

Proverbs 22:26-27 *Do not co-sign another person's note or put up a guarantee for someone else's loan. If you can't pay it, even your bed will be snatched from under you.*
If you co-sign a note, be absolutely sure you can repay the entire debt if your friend defaults on the loan. Otherwise, you will be putting yourself and your family at risk.

PROMISES FROM GOD

Philippians 4:19 *And this same God who takes care of me will supply all your needs from his glorious riches, which have been given to us in Christ Jesus.*

Hebrews 13:5 *Stay away from the love of money; be satisfied with what you have. For God has said, "I will never fail you. I will never forsake you."*

Forgiveness

(*see also* Grace, Guilt, Mercy)

There must be some sins that are too great for God to forgive. Can any sin be forgiven?

Mark 3:28 *I assure you that any sin can be forgiven.*

Romans 8:38 *Nothing can ever separate us from his love.*

Numbers 14:19 *Please pardon the sins of this people because of your magnificent, unfailing love, just as you have forgiven them ever since they left Egypt.*

Psalm 103:3, 10-12 *He forgives all my sins and heals all my diseases. . . . He has not punished us for all our sins, nor does he deal with us as we deserve. For his unfailing love toward those who fear him is as great as the height of the heavens above the earth. He has removed our rebellious acts as far away from us as the east is from the west.*

Forgiveness is not based on the magnitude of the sin, but the magnitude of the forgiver's love. No sin is too great for God's complete and unconditional love. The Bible does, however, mention one unforgivable sin—harboring an attitude of defiant hostility toward God that prevents us from accepting his forgiveness (see Mark 3:28-29 and Matthew 12:31). Only those who don't want God's forgiveness are out of its reach.

How can I forgive someone who has hurt me very badly?

Matthew 5:44 *Love your enemies! Pray for those who persecute you!*
Forgiveness means praying for those who hate you and hurt you.

Ephesians 4:31 *Get rid of all bitterness, rage, anger, harsh words, and slander, as well as all types of malicious behavior.*
Remember that unforgiveness not only ruins your relationships, but it also poisons your soul. The person most hurt by unforgiveness is you.

Ephesians 4:32 *Instead, be kind to one another, forgiving one another, just as God through Christ has forgiven you.*
God's forgiveness through Christ's death is the motivation and the model for your forgiveness of others. If God has forgiven you, how can you refuse to forgive someone who has wronged you? And your forgiveness, like God's, is a gift of grace, free to the recipient yet costly to the giver.

Romans 12:19 *Dear friends, never avenge yourselves. Leave that to God. For it is written, "I will take vengeance; I will repay those who deserve it," says the Lord.*
Punishing evildoers is God's job, not yours, and

God can be trusted to do his job. Therefore you can remove yourself from the endless cycle of revenge and retaliation by forgiving.

PROMISES FROM GOD
Isaiah 1:18 *No matter how deep the stain of your sins, I can remove it. I can make you as clean as freshly fallen snow.*

1 John 1:9 *But if we confess our sins to him, he is faithful and just to forgive us and to cleanse us from every wrong.*

Gossip

(*see also* Words)

Why is gossip so bad?
Leviticus 19:16 *Do not spread slanderous gossip among your people.*
Gossip is specifically forbidden by God.

Proverbs 11:13 *A gossip goes around revealing secrets, but those who are trustworthy can keep a confidence.*

Proverbs 18:8 *What dainty morsels rumors are—but they sink deep into one's heart.*
Gossips make poor friends. Gossips and trustworthy people work at opposite ends of the human spectrum. Trustworthy people build you

up. Gossips are demolition experts, trying to tear you down.

1 Timothy 5:13 *They are likely to become lazy and spend their time gossiping . . . , getting into other people's business and saying things they shouldn't.*
Gossiping often grows out of laziness. Gossips have nothing better to do than sit around talking about other people, saying things they might later regret.

How do I stop gossip?
Proverbs 26:20 *Fire goes out for lack of fuel, and quarrels disappear when gossip stops.*
Stop the chain of gossip with you! When you hear gossip you can do something about it. You can decide not to spread it any further.

Ephesians 4:29 *Let everything you say be good and helpful, so that your words will be an encouragement to those who hear them.*
If you focus on what is good and helpful, gossip will find no foothold in your heart.

Colossians 3:17 *And whatever you do or say, let it be as a representative of the Lord Jesus.*
If you think you may be about to gossip ask yourself, "Does the person I'm talking to need to know this? Is it true, accurate, and helpful?"

PROMISE FROM GOD
1 Peter 3:10 *For the Scriptures say, "If you want*

a happy life and good days, keep your tongue from speaking evil, and keep your lips from telling lies."

Grace

(*see also* Forgiveness, Mercy)

Where does grace come from? How do we receive it?

Psalm 84:11 *He gives us grace and glory. No good thing will the Lord withhold from those who do what is right.*

Romans 6:23 *For the wages of sin is death, but the free gift of God is eternal life through Christ Jesus our Lord.*

Ephesians 2:8 *God saved you by his special favor when you believed.*

Grace begins with God and is given freely by God. His graciousness to us is our example for extending grace and mercy to others. Grace cannot be earned. It is freely given.

Hebrews 4:16 *So let us come boldly to the throne of our gracious God. There we will receive his mercy, and we will find grace to help us when we need it.*

We may freely enter into God's presence, where he will freely give his mercy and grace.

PROMISES FROM GOD

Psalm 103:8   *The Lord is merciful and gracious; he is slow to get angry and full of unfailing love.*

Romans 6:14   *Sin is no longer your master, for you are no longer subject to the law, which enslaves you to sin. Instead, you are free by God's grace.*

Grief

(*see also* Brokenhearted, Encouragement, Suffering)

How does God minister to me in my grief?

Psalm 34:18   *The Lord is close to the broken-hearted; he rescues those who are crushed in spirit.*
God ministers to you through his comforting presence.

Psalm 10:14   *But you do see the trouble and grief they cause. You take note of it and punish them. The helpless put their trust in you. You are the defender of orphans.*
God ministers to you through his personal attention.

Psalm 119:28, 50, 52, 92   *I weep with grief; encourage me by your word. . . . Your promise revives me; it comforts me in all my troubles. . . . I meditate on your age-old laws; O Lord, they*

*comfort me. . . . If your law hadn't sustained me
with joy, I would have died in my misery.*
God ministers to you through his Word.

Romans 8:26-27 *And the Holy Spirit helps
us in our distress. For we don't even know what we
should pray for, nor how we should pray. But the
Holy Spirit prays for us with groanings that cannot
be expressed in words. And the Father who knows
all hearts knows what the Spirit is saying, for the
Spirit pleads for us believers in harmony with God's
own will.*
God ministers to you through his Spirit. When
you don't even know what to pray, the Holy
Spirit will pray for you.

Romans 8:28 *And we know that God causes
everything to work together for the good of those who
love God and are called according to his purpose for
them.*

Lamentations 3:32-33 *Though he brings
grief, he also shows compassion according to the
greatness of his unfailing love. For he does not enjoy
hurting people or causing them sorrow.*

John 16:20 *Truly, you will weep and mourn
over what is going to happen to me, but the world will
rejoice. You will grieve, but your grief will suddenly
turn to wonderful joy when you see me again.*
God ministers to you through his ultimate plan
for good.

Revelation 21:4 *He will remove all of their sorrows, and there will be no more death or sorrow or crying or pain. For the old world and its evils are gone forever.*
God ministers to you through his promise of eternity with him, free of all grief. When you lose perspective, ask God to show you a glimpse of eternity.

How can God use my grief for good?

James 4:9 *Let there be tears for the wrong things you have done. Let there be sorrow and deep grief. Let there be sadness instead of laughter, and gloom instead of joy.*
Your times of grief can lead to confession, repentance, and a restored relationship with God.

Lamentations 3:18-25 *I cry out, "My splendor is gone! Everything I had hoped for from the Lord is lost!" The thought of my suffering and homelessness is bitter beyond words. I will never forget this awful time, as I grieve over my loss. Yet I still dare to hope when I remember this: The unfailing love of the Lord never ends! By his mercies we have been kept from complete destruction. Great is his faithfulness; his mercies begin afresh each day. I say to myself, "The Lord is my inheritance; therefore, I will hope in him!" The Lord is wonderfully good to those who wait for him and seek him.*
Grief can renew your hope in God. In your grief,

dare to hope that the "unfailing love of the Lord never ends!"

Psalm 30:11-12 *You have turned my mourning into joyful dancing. You have taken away my clothes of mourning and clothed me with joy, that I might sing praises to you and not be silent. O Lord my God, I will give you thanks forever!*
Grief can lead to a time of praise and thanksgiving to God.

2 Corinthians 1:4-6 *He comforts us in all our troubles so that we can comfort others. When others are troubled, we will be able to give them the same comfort God has given us.*
Grief can help you have the compassion and capability to comfort others. Grief is a teacher, which helps you learn to relate to others who are grieving.

How did Jesus handle grief?

Luke 19:41-42 *But as they came closer to Jerusalem and Jesus saw the city ahead, he began to cry. "I wish that even today you would find the way of peace."*

Matthew 14:14 *A vast crowd was there as he stepped from the boat, and he had compassion on them and healed their sick.*

Mark 14:34 *He told them, "My soul is crushed with grief to the point of death. Stay here and watch with me."*

Isaiah 53:3-4, 10 *He was despised and rejected—a man of sorrows, acquainted with bitterest grief. We turned our backs on him and looked the other way when he went by. He was despised, and we did not care. Yet it was our weaknesses he carried; it was our sorrows that weighed him down. And we thought his troubles were a punishment from God for his own sins! . . . But it was the Lord's good plan to crush him and fill him with grief. Yet when his life is made an offering for sin, he will have a multitude of children, many heirs. He will enjoy a long life, and the Lord's plan will prosper in his hands.*

Jesus honestly expressed his emotions. At times Jesus wanted to be alone in his grief and at times he sought others to share in his grief. He did not let his circumstances or his feelings diminish his dedication to God. Jesus remained focused and committed to God.

PROMISE FROM GOD

Matthew 5:4 *God blesses those who mourn, for they will be comforted.*

Guidance

How can I be sure God will guide me?

Psalm 37:23 *The steps of the godly are directed by the Lord. He delights in every detail of their lives.*

Luke 12:6-7 *What is the price of five sparrows? A couple of pennies? Yet God does not forget a single one of them. And the very hairs on your head are all numbered. So don't be afraid; you are more valuable to him than a whole flock of sparrows.*

When you are anxious or concerned what you most often need is simply the assurance that God does indeed care about you and is watching over you. Jesus gives this promise to all his followers. If God values the little, most common things of his creation, how much more must he value you, for whom he gave his own precious Son?

How can I experience God's guidance?

Numbers 9:17 *When the cloud lifted from over the sacred tent, the people of Israel followed it.*

Proverbs 3:5-6 *Trust in the Lord with all your heart; do not depend on your own under- standing. Seek his will in all you do, and he will direct your paths.*

The first step in guidance is knowing where to put your trust. Travelers rely on an accurate map when they have never visited a place before. A critically ill person relies on the medical expert because he cannot treat himself. In the same way, you can trust God and realize your own limitations. You do not understand all the com- plexities of life, but the Lord does. Trust him to lead you.

Matthew 7:7-11 *Keep on asking, and you will be given what you ask for. Keep on looking, and you will find. Keep on knocking, and the door will be opened. For everyone who asks, receives. Everyone who seeks, finds. And the door is opened to everyone who knocks. You parents—if your children ask for a loaf of bread, do you give them a stone instead? Or if they ask for a fish, do you give them a snake? Of course not! If you sinful people know how to give good gifts to your children, how much more will your heavenly Father give good gifts to those who ask him.*

God invites you to pray so that you will know him more fully as your loving Father and understand yourself more clearly as well. Even as a parent gives more and more responsibility to a child as he or she grows, so the Lord expects you to take responsibility for seeking and following his direction.

PROMISES FROM GOD

Psalm 32:8 *I will guide you along the best pathway for your life. I will advise you and watch over you.*

Jeremiah 29:11 *"For I know the plans I have for you," says the Lord. "They are plans for good and not for disaster, to give you a future and a hope."*

Guilt

(*see also* Forgiveness, Grace, Mercy)

How can I be freed from guilt?

Numbers 14:40-41 *"We realize that we have sinned, but now we are ready to enter the land the Lord has promised us." But Moses said, ". . . It won't work."*

Jeremiah 3:13 *Only acknowledge your guilt. Admit that you rebelled against the Lord your God.* You must be sincere in admitting guilt. How can you deal with guilt if you deny that you have any sin?

Psalm 19:12-13 *Cleanse me from these hidden faults. Keep me from deliberate sins! Don't let them control me. Then I will be free of guilt.* You can be freed from guilt by avoiding sin as much as possible and confessing any sin to God. Guilt is the consequence of wrongdoing.

Job 6:29 *Stop assuming my guilt.* Job's friends kept assuming he was guilty for some sin that caused his trouble. Sometimes you are not guilty of wrongdoing, but you feel guilty. You must learn to discern between true and false guilt.

How do I handle lingering guilt feelings, even after I have confessed my sin?

Acts 13:39 *Everyone who believes in him is freed from all guilt and declared right with God.*

1 John 1:9 *But if we confess our sins to him, he is faithful and just to forgive us and to cleanse us from every wrong.*

Psalm 51:7 *Purify me from my sins, and I will be clean; wash me, and I will be whiter than snow.* Sometimes the hardest thing is to believe the good news. You need to trust God's truth, not your fickle, fluctuating feelings. Most of your guilt is really shame and regret over what you have done. Along with confessing your sins, you need to claim (or agree with) God's promise to forgive you and cleanse you.

PROMISE FROM GOD

Romans 8:1 *So now there is no condemnation for those who belong to Christ Jesus.*

Romans 3:23-24 *For all have sinned; all fall short of God's glorious standard. Yet now God in his gracious kindness declares us not guilty. He has done this through Christ Jesus, who has freed us by taking away our sins.*

Hand of God

What does God's hand bring to me here in this world today?

James 1:17 *Whatever is good and perfect comes to us from God above, who created all heaven's lights.*

96

Everything good and perfect comes from God's hand.

Job 2:10 *But Job replied, ". . . Should we accept only good things from the hand of God and never anything bad?"*
Sometimes God allows bad things to happen to good people. Why? Because his long-range eternal plans for our greater good may not fit our short-range view of comfort.

Ecclesiastes 2:24 *So I decided there is nothing better than to enjoy food and drink and to find satisfaction in work. Then I realized that this pleasure is from the hand of God.*
The pleasure of God's provision transcends the pleasure of the provisions themselves. For example, God's gift of bread is far more pleasurable than the taste of bread itself.

How can I remember God's hand in past events of my life?

Psalm 103:2 *Praise the Lord, I tell myself, and never forget the good things he does for me.*
Through praise for God's wonderful work, you can reinforce the memory of that work.

Psalm 106:2 *Who can list the glorious miracles of the Lord? Who can ever praise him half enough?*
To recite God's miracles in your life is to recall and reinforce the impact of those miracles.

Psalm 145:5 *I will meditate on your majesty,*
glorious splendor and your wonderful miracles.
Meditating on God's work in your life helps you
remember all he has done for you.

Psalm 71:18 *Now that I am old and gray, do*
not abandon me, O God. Let me proclaim your power
to this new generation, your mighty miracles to all
who come after me.

Psalm 78:4 *We will not hide these truths from*
our children.

Psalm 105:2 *Sing to him; yes, sing his praises.*
Tell everyone about his miracles.
Sharing God's miracles with children, grandchil-
dren, and others builds a heritage for future
generations.

PROMISE FROM GOD
Psalm 40:5 *O Lord my God, you have done*
many miracles for us. Your plans for us are too numer-
ous to list. If I tried to recite all your wonderful deeds,
I would never come to the end of them.

Healing

(*see also* Health, Miracles)

How does God heal?
2 Kings 20:7 *"Make an ointment from figs and*

spread it over the boil." They did this, and Hezekiah recovered!
Through physicians and medicine.

Psalm 119:93   *I will never forget your commandments, for you have used them to restore my joy and health.*
Through his Word.

Luke 5:12-13   *"Lord," he said, "if you want to, you can make me well again." Jesus reached out and touched the man. "I want to," he said. "Be healed!"*
Through miracles.

Mark 2:4-5   *They couldn't get to Jesus through the crowd, so they dug through the clay roof above his head. . . . Seeing their faith, Jesus said to the paralyzed man, "My son, your sins are forgiven."*
Through the faith of friends.

Psalm 6:2   *Heal me, Lord, for my body is in agony.*

James 5:14   *Are any among you sick? They should call for the elders of the church and have them pray over them.*
Through prayer.

Isaiah 38:16   *Lord, your discipline is good, for it leads to life and health.*
Through discipline.

Genesis 27:41; 33:4   *Esau hated Jacob. . . . Then Esau ran to meet [Jacob] and embraced him*

*affectionately and kissed him. Both of them were
in tears.*
Through time.

Isaiah 53:5   *He was wounded and crushed for
our sins. He was beaten that we might have peace.
He was whipped, and we were healed!*
Through Christ. His death brought you life; his
wounds brought you healing. By accepting your
punishment he set you free.

Revelation 21:4   *He will remove all of their
sorrows, and there will be no more death or sorrow
or crying or pain. For the old world and its evils are
gone forever.*
Through his promise of heaven, for there you will
receive complete and final healing.

Why doesn't God always heal people?

Psalm 103:2-3   *Praise the Lord, I tell myself,
and never forget the good things he does for me. He
forgives all my sins and heals all my diseases.*

Matthew 4:23-24   *Jesus traveled throughout
Galilee teaching in the synagogues, preaching every-
where the Good News about the Kingdom. And he
healed people who had every kind of sickness and
disease. News about him spread far beyond the
borders of Galilee so that the sick were soon coming
to be healed from as far away as Syria. And whatever
their illness and pain, or if they were possessed by*

demons, or were epileptics, or were paralyzed—
he healed them all.

Our compassionate, merciful God has full authority over all sickness. He can heal whomever he
chooses. He can grant his authority to heal to
whomever he chooses. But why he heals some
and not others is not known to us. Eventually,
we do know that he will remove all sickness and
suffering from all of his children for eternity.
We will live in heaven forever where there will
be no sickness or disease (see Revelation 21:4).

2 C o r i n t h i a n s 1 2 : 9 *My power works best*
in your weakness.

We do not know why God heals some people
and not others. But we do know that God's
power is magnified through our weaknesses and
infirmities if we allow him to work within us. If
you have been praying to be healed—or praying
for a loved one to be healed—and God has not
done it, trust that he has something even greater
that he wants to do through the illness.

P s a l m 7 3 : 2 4 - 2 6 *You will keep on guiding me*
with your counsel, leading me to a glorious destiny.
Whom have I in heaven but you? I desire you more
than anything on earth. My health may fail, and my
spirit may grow weak, but God remains the strength
of my heart; he is mine forever.

Whether or not God chooses to heal us physically,
we can have the unspeakable gift of knowing him

personally. His love and the promise of eternal life with him are our greatest sources comfort and hope.

How do I deal with it if I'm not healed on earth?

2 Corinthians 12:10 *Since I know it is all for Christ's good, I am quite content with my weaknesses.* You can look forward to having God's power work through you in a special way despite your weaknesses. When God works through your weaknesses, it is obvious that what occurred happened because of him, thus showing the world his love and power.

PROMISES FROM GOD

Psalm 147:3 *He heals the brokenhearted, binding up their wounds.*

Malachi 4:2 *But for you who fear my name, the Sun of Righteousness will rise with healing in his wings. And you will go free, leaping with joy like calves let out to pasture.*

Health

(*see also* Healing)

Why do we get sick?

1 Corinthians 15:43 *Our bodies now disap-*

point us, but when they are raised, they will be full of glory. They are weak now, but when they are raised, they will be full of power.

Our physical bodies are victim to physical ailments.

How do I find rest in times of poor health?

Psalm 73:26 *My health may fail, and my spirit may grow weak, but God remains the strength of my heart; he is mine forever.*

Whether you have good health or poor health, you must rely on God for strength of spirit. He gives you the strength to hold on to your hope of eternal life where there will be no more health problems!

What is my responsibility toward those who are sick?

Galatians 4:14 *Even though my sickness was revolting to you, you did not reject me and turn me away.*

Sickness in a friend or loved one may be unpleasant, but that is no reason to reject anyone. It is easy to stay away from older family members when their health fails. Don't miss the ministry opportunities sickness brings.

PROMISES FROM GOD

Proverbs 17:22 *A cheerful heart is good medicine, but a broken spirit saps a person's strength.*

Isaiah 58:11 *The Lord will guide you continually, watering your life when you are dry and keeping you healthy, too. You will be like a well-watered garden, like an ever-flowing spring.*

Heaven

What is heaven like?

Isaiah 65:17 *Look! I am creating new heavens and a new earth—so wonderful that no one will even think about the old ones anymore.*

Philippians 3:21 *He will take these weak mortal bodies of ours and change them into glorious bodies like his own.*

Revelation 21:3-4 *I heard a loud shout from the throne, saying, "Look, the home of God is now among his people! He will live with them, and they will be his people. God himself will be with them. He will remove all of their sorrows, and there will be no more death or sorrow or crying or pain. For the old world and its evils are gone forever."*

Revelation 22:5 *And there will be no night there—no need for lamps or sun—for the Lord God will shine on them. And they will reign forever and ever.*

Heaven is far beyond anything we can imagine. In heaven we will live forever with God. There will be no sadness, no pain, no evil, no death. Everything will be perfect and glorious. God will give us new bodies and we will be able to talk face-to-face with the Lord himself.

Who will get into heaven?

Matthew 5:3 *God blesses those who realize their need for him, for the Kingdom of Heaven is given to them.*

Matthew 19:14 *But Jesus said, "Let the children come to me. Don't stop them! For the Kingdom of Heaven belongs to such as these."*

John 3:16 *For God so loved the world that he gave his only Son, so that everyone who believes in him will not perish but have eternal life.*

John 14:6 *Jesus told him, "I am the way, the truth, and the life. No one can come to the Father except through me."*

Those who accept Jesus Christ as Savior and recognize that only he can forgive their sins will gain entrance into heaven. This only occurs with a humble and repentant attitude.

How can I be sure I will go to heaven?

Romans 8:38-39 *I am convinced that nothing can ever separate us from his love. Death can't, and life can't. The angels can't, and the demons can't. Our fears for today, our worries about tomorrow, and even the powers of hell can't keep God's love away.*

Whether we are high above the sky or in the deepest ocean, nothing in all creation will ever be able to separate us from the love of God that is revealed in Christ Jesus our Lord.

God's love is stronger than any person, supernatural foe, or circumstance that may threaten us. No matter what comes your way, nothing can separate you from God's love when you trust in Jesus Christ.

PROMISES FROM GOD

John 14:2 *There are many rooms in my Father's home, and I am going to prepare a place for you.*

1 Corinthians 2:9 *No eye has seen, no ear has heard, and no mind has imagined what God has prepared for those who love him.*

Revelation 3:5 *All who are victorious will be clothed in white. I will never erase their names from the Book of Life.*

Hopelessness

How can God help me handle times of hopelessness?

Psalm 10:17 *Lord, you know the hopes of the helpless. Surely you will listen to their cries and comfort them.*

Psalm 40:2 *He lifted me out of the pit of despair, out of the mud and the mire. He set my feet on solid ground and steadied me as I walked along.*
You can find hope in God's loving care for you, for he knows, listens, heals, and helps.

2 Samuel 24:14 *"This is a desperate situation!" David replied to Gad. "But let us fall into the hands of the Lord, for his mercy is great. Do not let me fall into human hands."*

Psalm 40:11 *Lord, don't hold back your tender mercies from me. My only hope is in your unfailing love and faithfulness.*
You can find hope in God's character, for he alone is loving, faithful, and merciful.

Psalm 119:43, 49, 74, 81 *Do not snatch your word of truth from me, for my only hope is in your laws. . . . Remember your promise to me, for it is my only hope. . . . May all who fear you find in me a cause for joy, for I have put my hope in your word. . . I faint with longing for your salvation; but I have put my hope in your word.*
You can find hope in God's Word, for only there are the promises of God.

Mark 10:27 *Jesus looked at them intently and said, "Humanly speaking, it is impossible. But not with God. Everything is possible with God."*
You can find hope in remembering that God specializes in the impossible!

How can I maintain hope in discouraging circumstances?

Daniel 2:18-19 *He urged them to ask the God of heaven to show them his mercy by telling them the secret, so they would not be executed along with the other wise men of Babylon. That night the secret was revealed to Daniel in a vision. Then Daniel praised the God of heaven.*
Don't panic! Start praying. You'll discover God's presence.

Isaiah 26:3 *You will keep in perfect peace all who trust in you, whose thoughts are fixed on you!*
Focus on God. Keep praying. You'll discover God's peace.

Romans 12:12 *Be glad for all God is planning for you. Be patient in trouble, and always be prayerful.*
Remember that God is sovereign and loving. Be patient and prayerful. You'll discover the joy of knowing he cares for you.

Romans 15:4 *Such things were written in the Scriptures long ago to teach us. They give us hope and encouragement as we wait patiently for God's promises.*
Read God's Word. Learn how to apply it to your life. You'll discover the power of God's promises.

Psalm 62:5 *I wait quietly before God, for my hope is in him.*

Psalm 27:14 *Wait patiently for the Lord. Be brave and courageous. Yes, wait patiently for the Lord.*

Wait quietly and patiently for God to work. You'll discover he always comes through.

PROMISES FROM GOD

Jeremiah 29:11 *"For I know the plans I have for you," says the Lord. "They are plans for good and not for disaster, to give you a future and a hope."*

Psalm 43:5 *Why am I discouraged? Why so sad? I will put my hope in God! I will praise him again—my Savior and my God!*

Hurts/Hurting

(*see also* Grief, Suffering)

When I've been hurt, how can I find healing?

Ecclesiastes 3:4 *A time to cry and a time to laugh. A time to grieve and a time to dance.*

2 Corinthians 2:4 *How painful it was to write that letter! Heartbroken, I cried over it. I didn't want to hurt you, but I wanted you to know how very much I love you.*

Acts 20:37 *They wept aloud as they embraced him in farewell.*

2 Samuel 18:33 *The king was overcome with emotion. He went up to his room over the gateway and burst into tears. And as he went, he cried, "O my son Absalom! My son, my son Absalom! If only I could have died instead of you! O Absalom, my son, my son."*
You need to express your pain—privately to God, to a friend, or even publicly. Unexpressed pain can fester within you, driving you toward many unwanted emotions like depression or bitterness.

Psalm 34:18 *The Lord is close to the broken-hearted; he rescues those who are crushed in spirit.*

Isaiah 51:12 *I, even I, am the one who comforts you. So why are you afraid of mere humans, who wither like the grass and disappear?*
God compassionately cares for you. Meditate on the attributes of his character and recognize that the one who made you is the best one to heal you.

Psalm 119:28, 50, 52, 92 *I weep with grief; encourage me by your word. . . . Your promise revives me; it comforts me in all my troubles. . . . I meditate on your age-old laws; O Lord, they comfort me. . . . If your law hadn't sustained me with joy, I would have died in my misery.*
Look to God's Word, the Bible, as a source of comfort and healing. These are the words of God himself, and there is much there about turning your hurts into healing.

Romans 8:23 *And even we Christians, although we have the Holy Spirit within us as a foretaste of future glory, also groan to be released from pain and suffering. We, too, wait anxiously for that day when God will give us our full rights as his children, including the new bodies he has promised us.*

God does not promise believers a life without pain or suffering. If Christians didn't hurt, people would turn to God as a magic potion to take away their pain. The difference is that Christians have a relationship with God that helps us through our hurts, comforts us in our hurts, and sometimes miraculously heals our hurts. But most important, we have a God who will one day take away all of our hurts when we arrive at heaven's doorstep. Whatever pain you are experiencing is temporal; it will end.

Genesis 33:4 *Then Esau ran to meet him and embraced him affectionately and kissed him. Both of them were in tears.*

Forgiveness is like a miracle medicine to heal our brokenness. Extend and accept it gladly.

How should I respond to those who hurt me?

Matthew 18:20-21 *Then Peter came to him and asked, "Lord, how often should I forgive someone who sins against me? Seven times?" "No!" Jesus replied, "seventy times seven!"*

Mark 11:25 *But when you are praying, first forgive anyone you are holding a grudge against, so that your Father in heaven will forgive your sins, too.* Forgiveness is not an option; it is a command. It is necessary for the health of your own relationship with God. Jesus gave us the perfect example of forgiveness to follow. Forgiveness doesn't mean you say that the hurt doesn't exist or that it doesn't matter, nor does it make everything "all right." Forgiveness allows you to let go of the anger at the one who hurt you and let God deal with him or her. Forgiveness sets you free. Forgiveness allows you to put the past in the past and move on with your life. It won't be easy, but forgiving the hurts others have caused you is the most healthy act you can do for yourself.

Proverbs 20:22 *Don't say, "I will get even for this wrong." Wait for the Lord to handle the matter.*

1 Peter 3:8-9 *Finally, all of you should be of one mind, full of sympathy toward each other, loving one another with tender hearts and humble minds. Don't repay evil for evil. Don't retaliate when people say unkind things about you. Instead, pay them back with a blessing. That is what God wants you to do, and he will bless you for it.*
You must wait for the Lord to do things his way. God wants you to respond in love with a blessing rather than retaliation.

Colossians 3:13 *You must make allowance for each other's faults and forgive the person who offends you. Remember, the Lord forgave you, so you must forgive others.*

1 Corinthians 13:5 *Love does not demand its own way. Love is not irritable, and it keeps no record of when it has been wronged.*

You can sometimes avoid being hurt by being less sensitive to others' faults, offenses and wrongs toward you.

PROMISES FROM GOD

Psalm 121:4-7 *Indeed, he who watches over Israel never tires and never sleeps. The Lord himself watches over you! The Lord stands beside you as your protective shade. The sun will not hurt you by day, nor the moon at night. The Lord keeps you from all evil and preserves your life.*

Revelation 21:4 *He will remove all of their sorrows, and there will be no more death or sorrow or crying or pain. For the old world and its evils are gone forever.*

Incest

How can God allow incest? Why doesn't he stop it?

Romans 1:24-26 *So God let them go ahead and do whatever shameful things their hearts desired.*

As a result, they did vile and degrading things with each other's bodies. Instead of believing what they knew was the truth about God, they deliberately chose to believe lies. . . . That is why God abandoned them to their shameful desires.

1 Thessalonians 4 : 3 - 5 *God wants you to be holy, so you should keep clear of all sexual sin. Then each of you will control your body and live in holiness and honor—not in lustful passion as the pagans do, in their ignorance of God and his ways.*

Leviticus 18 : 6 *You must never have sexual intercourse with a close relative, for I am the Lord.*

Mark 7 : 20 - 21 *For from within, out of a person's heart, come evil thoughts, sexual immorality, theft, murder, adultery, greed, wickedness, deceit, eagerness for lustful pleasure, envy, slander, pride, and foolishness.*

Jude 1 : 7 *And don't forget the cities of Sodom and Gomorrah and their neighboring towns, which were filled with sexual immorality and every kind of sexual perversion. Those cities were destroyed by fire and are a warning of the eternal fire that will punish all who are evil.*

God allows free choice and clearly warns us to stay away from all sexual immorality. God never chooses sin for us but gives us the freedom to choose it or reject it. Incest, like every other vile sin, is the result of evil choices by fallen human

114

beings who are far from God. God is aware of it, is angered by it, and will see that justice prevails.

Although I am the victim of incest, I feel so ashamed and so angry. How can I ever recover?

Psalm 18:21-24, 26 *For I have kept the ways of the Lord; I have not turned from my God to follow evil. For all his laws are constantly before me; I have never abandoned his principles. I am blameless before God; I have kept myself from sin. The Lord rewarded me for doing right, because of the innocence of my hands in his sight. . . . To the pure you show yourself pure, but to the wicked you show yourself hostile.*
You are a victim, not the perpetrator. God is not hostile toward you. God draws near the wounded to offer healing.

Romans 15:16 *I bring you the Good News and offer you up as a fragrant sacrifice to God so that you might be pure and pleasing to him by the Holy Spirit.*

1 Corinthians 1:30 *God alone made it possible for you to be in Christ Jesus. For our benefit God made Christ to be wisdom itself. He is the one who made us acceptable to God. He made us pure and holy, and he gave himself to purchase our freedom.*
You are pure and holy because of Christ Jesus. He does not see you as violated, but as whole.

Could God forgive me if I've been the perpetrator?

Psalm 51:1-4, 10, 12, 17 *Have mercy on me, O God, because of your unfailing love. Because of your great compassion, blot out the stain of my sins. Wash me clean from my guilt. Purify me from my sin. For I recognize my shameful deeds—they haunt me day and night. Against you, and you alone, have I sinned; I have done what is evil in your sight. You will be proved right in what you say, and your judgment against me is just. . . . Create in me a clean heart, O God. Renew a right spirit within me. . . . Restore to me again the joy of your salvation, and make me willing to obey you. . . . The sacrifice you want is a broken spirit. A broken and repentant heart, O God, you will not despise.*

You must first agree with God that you have sinned; there is no excuse and no exception. You must then realize how shameful your sin has been, and how ugly sin has made you on the inside. Only then can you sincerely beg for God's mercy and forgiveness. You do this by being truly sorry for your sin, confessing your sin to God, and asking for forgiveness, which he will give you.

2 Corinthians 12:21 *Yes, I am afraid that when I come, God will humble me again because of you. And I will have to grieve because many of you who sinned earlier have not repented of their impurity, sexual immorality, and eagerness for lustful pleasure.*

1 Peter 4:2-3 *And you won't spend the rest of your life chasing after evil desires, but you will be anxious to do the will of God. You have had enough in the past of the evil things that godless people enjoy—their immorality and lust, their feasting and drunkenness and wild parties, and their terrible worship of idols.*

True confession must be accompanied by repentance, a commitment to turn sharply away from your sinful lifestyle and toward a life that honors God and others. You can only do this by the power of God's Holy Spirit at work within you. The way of repentance leads to godliness and hope for a new start.

1 John 1:9 *But if we confess our sins to him, he is faithful and just to forgive us and to cleanse us from every wrong.*

1 Corinthians 6:9-11 *Don't you know that those who do wrong will have no share in the Kingdom of God? Don't fool yourselves. Those who indulge in sexual sin, who are idol worshipers, adulterers, male prostitutes, homosexuals, thieves, greedy people, drunkards, abusers, and swindlers—none of these will have a share in the Kingdom of God. There was a time when some of you were just like that, but now your sins have been washed away, and you have been set apart for God. You have been made right with God because of what the Lord Jesus Christ and the Spirit of our God have done for you.*

Finally, accept God's forgiveness and move forward in obedience to him. And don't look back. Half-hearted repentance is no repentance at all.

PROMISES FROM GOD

Psalm 147:3 *He heals the brokenhearted, binding up their wounds.*

Romans 13:13-14 *We should be decent and true in everything we do, so that everyone can approve of our behavior. Don't participate in wild parties and getting drunk, or in adultery and immoral living. . . . But let the Lord Jesus Christ take control of you, and don't think of ways to indulge your evil desires.*

2 Timothy 2:22 *Run from anything that stimulates youthful lust. Follow anything that makes you want to do right. Pursue faith and love and peace, and enjoy the companionship of those who call on the Lord with pure hearts.*

Injustice

Why does a loving, sovereign God allow injustice? Why doesn't he stop it?

Psalm 9:16 *The Lord is known for his justice. The wicked have trapped themselves in their own snares.*

Ezekiel 9:9-10 *Then he said to me, "The sins of the people of Israel and Judah are very great. The entire land is full of murder; the city is filled with injustice. They are saying, 'The Lord doesn't see it! The Lord has forsaken the land!' So I will not spare them or have any pity on them. I will fully repay them for all they have done."*

Job 35:14 *And it is even more false to say he doesn't see what is going on. He will bring about justice if you will only wait.*

2 Chronicles 19:7 *Fear the Lord and judge with care, for the Lord our God does not tolerate perverted justice, partiality, or the taking of bribes.*

Job 36:6, 17 *He does not let the wicked live but gives justice to the afflicted. . . . But you are too obsessed with judgment on the godless. Don't worry, justice will be upheld.*

Injustice happens because God created human beings with free will—we have the freedom to choose good or evil, right or wrong. If God hadn't done it that way, we would only be puppets of a divine dictator, not people who love him. God knew that people needed the freedom to choose, but that also means that many will choose wrongly, causing injustice to the innocent. But to think that God condones injustice simply because it happens is contrary to his righteous nature and opposed to what the Bible teaches about all sin. God sees every injustice, and judges it to be sin.

How should I respond to personal injustice?

Psalm 17:1 *O Lord, hear my plea for justice. Listen to my cry for help. Pay attention to my prayer, for it comes from an honest heart.*

Too often we tell everyone about our injustice except God. Go to God in honest prayer. Ask him for justice.

Proverbs 20:22 *Don't say, "I will get even for this wrong." Wait for the Lord to handle the matter.*

Wait patiently for God to work; take no revenge. You won't always understand God's timing, but you can trust it to be right.

Matthew 5:39-45 *But I say, don't resist an evil person! If you are slapped on the right cheek, turn the other, too. If you are ordered to court and your shirt is taken from you, give your coat, too. If a soldier demands that you carry his gear for a mile, carry it two miles. Give to those who ask, and don't turn away from those who want to borrow. You have heard that the law of Moses says, "Love your neighbor" and hate your enemy. But I say, love your enemies! Pray for those who persecute you! In that way, you will be acting as true children of your Father in heaven. For he gives his sunlight to both the evil and the good, and he sends rain on the just and on the unjust, too.*

Love your enemy. Practically, begin by praying for the person inflicting injustice on you. At the very least, praying for your enemy might not change your enemy but it will change you.

1 Peter 3:14 *But even if you suffer for doing what is right, God will reward you for it. So don't be afraid and don't worry.*

Do not allow fear and worry to overcome you, lest you double the burden of injustice.

Matthew 27:12-14 *But when the leading priests and other leaders made their accusations against him, Jesus remained silent. "Don't you hear their many charges against you?" Pilate demanded. But Jesus said nothing, much to the governor's great surprise.*

Luke 12:11-12 *And when you are brought to trial in the synagogues and before rulers and authorities, don't worry about what to say in your defense, for the Holy Spirit will teach you what needs to be said even as you are standing there.*

Look to God for guidance as to when to speak and what to say.

1 Corinthians 6:7 *To have such lawsuits at all is a real defeat for you. Why not just accept the injustice and leave it at that? Why not let yourselves be cheated?*

1 Peter 2:19 *For God is pleased with you when, for the sake of your conscience, you patiently endure unfair treatment.*

Be willing to endure the earthly injustice. Some things will not change until we get to heaven and ultimate justice is determined. You may be a victim of earthly injustice. If you are, then the real test is how you react to it as a Christian.

Psalm 37:34 *Don't be impatient for the Lord to act! Travel steadily along his path. He will honor you, giving you the land. You will see the wicked destroyed.*

Isaiah 56:1 *"Be just and fair to all," says the Lord. "Do what is right and good, for I am coming soon to rescue you."*

1 Peter 2:12, 15 *Be careful how you live among your unbelieving neighbors. Even if they accuse you of doing wrong, they will see your honorable behavior, and they will believe and give honor to God when he comes to judge the world. . . . It is God's will that your good lives should silence those who make foolish accusations against you.*
Continue on in obedience to God and his Word.

Genesis 45:4-8 *"Come over here," he said. So they came closer. And he said again, "I am Joseph, your brother whom you sold into Egypt. But don't be angry with yourselves that you did this to me, for God did it. He sent me here ahead of you to preserve your lives. These two years of famine will grow to seven, during which there will be neither plowing nor harvest. God has sent me here to keep you and your families alive so that you will become a great nation. Yes, it was God who sent me here, not you! And he has made me a counselor to Pharaoh—manager of his entire household and ruler over all Egypt."*

Psalm 101:1 *I will sing of your love and justice. I will praise you, Lord, with songs.*
Allow God to work, look for God at work, and acknowledge God's work.

PROMISES FROM GOD
Job 34:12 *There is no truer statement than this: God will not do wrong. The Almighty cannot twist justice.*

Psalm 103:6 *The Lord gives righteousness and justice to all who are treated unfairly.*

Psalm 106:3 *Happy are those who deal justly with others and always do what is right.*

Insignificance

(*see also* Self-Esteem, Worth/Worthiness)

How can I cope with feelings of insignificance?

Psalm 8:4-5 *What are mortals that you should think of us, mere humans that you should care for us? For you made us only a little lower than God, and you crowned us with glory and honor.*
The Creator of the universe considers you significant.

Galatians 2:20 *The Son of God . . . loved me and gave himself for me.*

God thinks you're worthy, so much so that he gave his Son for you.

Matthew 10:29-31 *Not even a sparrow, worth only half a penny, can fall to the ground without your Father knowing it. And the very hairs on your head are all numbered. So don't be afraid; you are more valuable to him than a whole flock of sparrows.*
You matter to God. God thinks every event and detail of your life is important.

Do I have to be important for God to use me?

1 Corinthians 1:26-27 *Remember, dear brothers and sisters, that few of you were wise in the world's eyes, or powerful, or wealthy when God called you. Instead, God deliberately chose things the world considers foolish in order to shame those who think they are wise. And he chose those who are powerless to shame those who are powerful.*
Significance in the eyes of the world may be insignificance in God's eyes. Insignificance in the world's eyes may be significance in God's eyes. God takes joy in choosing people the world considers "insignificant" to accomplish marvelous things for his Kingdom.

PROMISE FROM GOD
Zechariah 4:10 *Do not despise these small beginnings, for the Lord rejoices to see the work begin.*

Insults

How am I to respond to insults?

1 Samuel 10:26-27 *When Saul returned to his home at Gibeah, a band of men whose hearts God had touched became his constant companions. But there were some wicked men who complained, "How can this man save us?" And they despised him and refused to bring him gifts. But Saul ignored them.*

Acts 18:6 *But when the Jews opposed him and insulted him, Paul shook the dust from his robe and said, "Your blood be upon your own heads—I am innocent. From now on I will go to the Gentiles."*

Proverbs 12:16 *A fool is quick-tempered, but a wise person stays calm when insulted.*

Sometimes it is best to ignore insults, and other times you must respond. When you do respond to insults, you should do so in a deliberate, controlled, and loving manner. All of your responses should be bathed in prayer, as you trust in God for the right words.

Luke 6:22-23 *God blesses you who are hated and excluded and mocked and cursed because you are identified with me, the Son of Man. When that happens, rejoice! Yes, leap for joy! For a great reward awaits you in heaven. And remember, the ancient prophets were also treated that way by your ancestors.*

2 Corinthians 12:10 *Since I know it is all for Christ's good, I am quite content with my weaknesses and with insults, hardships, persecutions, and calamities. For when I am weak, then I am strong.*

Hebrews 10:32-34 *Don't ever forget those early days when you first learned about Christ. Remember how you remained faithful even though it meant terrible suffering. Sometimes you were exposed to public ridicule and were beaten, and sometimes you helped others who were suffering the same things. You suffered along with those who were thrown into jail. When all you owned was taken from you, you accepted it with joy. You knew you had better things waiting for you in eternity.*

1 Peter 4:14 *Be happy if you are insulted for being a Christian, for then the glorious Spirit of God will come upon you.*

Keep an eternal perspective regarding insults. Rejoice in the midst of temporary insults when you are insulted for Jesus' sake, for you know that in the end you will be victorious with him.

Lamentations 3:25-31, 61 *The Lord is wonderfully good to those who wait for him and seek him. So it is good to wait quietly for salvation from the Lord. . . . Let them turn the other cheek to those who strike them. Let them accept the insults of their enemies. For the Lord does not abandon anyone forever. . . . Lord, you have heard the vile names they call me. You know all about the plans they have made.*

The Lord is aware of any insult that is hurled
against you. He will comfort you when insulted
and reward you for the way in which you
respond. And eventually, you will enter a place
where there will be no more insults.

PROMISE FROM GOD
Job 5:15   *He rescues the poor from the cutting
words of the strong. He saves them from the clutches
of the powerful.*

Joy

How can I more fully experience joy?

Psalm 70:4   *But may all who search for you be
filled with joy and gladness. May those who love your
salvation repeatedly shout, "God is great!"*
Actively pursue knowing God as the priority of
your life. The more you know God, the creator
of joy, the more you will know joy!

Psalm 28:7   *The Lord is my strength, my shield
from every danger. I trust in him with all my heart.
He helps me, and my heart is filled with joy. I burst
out in songs of thanksgiving.*
A growing faith and trust in God is vital to experiencing joy in every situation. Joy overflows from
the fullness of your faith and trust in the Lord of
all joy.

Psalm 119:1-2, 14, 16, 24 *Happy are people of integrity, who follow the law of the Lord. Happy are those who obey his decrees and search for him with all their hearts. . . . I have rejoiced in your decrees as much as in riches. . . . I will delight in your principles and not forget your word. . . . Your decrees please me; they give me wise advice.*

Psalm 19:8 *The commandments of the Lord are right, bringing joy to the heart. The commands of the Lord are clear, giving insight to life.*
Read, study, and follow God's Word, for in it you find the key to real joy.

Proverbs 13:9 *The life of the godly is full of light and joy, but the sinner's light is snuffed out.*

Galatians 5:22-23 *But when the Holy Spirit controls our lives, he will produce this kind of fruit in us: love, joy, peace, patience, kindness, goodness, faithfulness, gentleness, and self-control. Here there is no conflict with the law.*

Romans 14:17 *For the Kingdom of God is not a matter of what we eat or drink, but of living a life of goodness and peace and joy in the Holy Spirit.*
Live in obedience to God through the power of his Holy Spirit, because one of the fruits of the Spirit is joy.

2 John 12 *Well, I have much more to say to you, but I don't want to say it in a letter. For I hope to visit*

you soon and to talk with you face to face. Then our joy will be complete.

A c t s   2 : 4 6   *They worshiped together at the Temple each day, met in homes for the Lord's Supper, and shared their meals with great joy and generosity.*
Be with other believers. Joy is a shared blessing from others who have tasted the fruit of the Spirit.

PROMISES FROM GOD
P s a l m   1 6 : 1 1   *You will show me the way of life, granting me the joy of your presence and the pleasures of living with you forever.*

P s a l m   6 9 : 3 2   *The humble will see their God at work and be glad. Let all who seek God's help live in joy.*

Loneliness

(*see also* Abandonment, Neglect)

Has everyone deserted me?
E x o d u s   6 : 1 2   *"But Lord!" Moses objected. "My own people won't listen to me anymore."*

P s a l m   2 7 : 1 0   *Even if my father and mother abandon me, the Lord will hold me close.*

P r o v e r b s   1 8 : 2 4   *There are "friends" who destroy each other, but a real friend sticks closer than a brother.*

Deuteronomy 33:27 *The eternal God is your refuge, and his everlasting arms are under you. He thrusts out the enemy before you.*

Hebrews 13:5 *God has said, "I will never fail you. I will never forsake you."*
People we depend on sometimes desert us, abandon us, or turn away from us. There may be only a few people you can truly count on—at times there may not be any. But you can always count on God; he will never abandon you.

How can God help me with my loneliness?

Psalm 23:4 *Even when I walk through the dark valley of death, . . . you are close beside me.*

Psalm 139:17 *How precious are your thoughts about me, O God!*

Isaiah 54:10 *For the mountains may depart and the hills disappear, but even then I will remain loyal to you.*
Recognize that you are not unlovable or deficient just because you are lonely. You have value because God made you, loves you, and promises never to leave you.

Exodus 5:21-22 *The foremen said to them, "May the Lord judge you for getting us into this terrible situation. . . ." So Moses went back to the Lord and protested, ". . . Why did you send me?"*

1 Kings 19:4, 10 *He sat down under a solitary*

broom tree and prayed that he might die. . . . "I alone am left, and now they are trying to kill me, too."
Don't give up on God when you are lonely. It will cause you to feel sorry for yourself, become discouraged, and fall prey to temptation. Be careful that in your loneliness you do not separate yourself from the One who wants to be with you always.

Hebrews 10:25 *And let us not neglect our meeting together, as some people do, but encourage and warn each other, especially now that the day of his coming back again is drawing near.*
The best way to avoid loneliness is to get together with other believers. Get involved in a local church. Get busy with God's people doing God's work.

Isaiah 41:10 *Don't be afraid, for I am with you. Do not be dismayed, for I am your God. I will strengthen you. I will help you. I will uphold you with my victorious right hand.*
Loneliness can cause you to be afraid. Trust God and let him calm your fears.

PROMISE FROM GOD
Romans 12:5 *We are all parts of his one body, and each of us has different work to do. And since we are all one body in Christ, we belong to each other, and each of us needs all the others.*

Loss

(*see also* Death, Sympathy)

How do I deal with loss in my life?

John 11:35 *Then Jesus wept.*
The tears of Jesus at Lazarus's death forever validate our tears of grief. Don't deny your loss. Great grief is the result of great love.

Genesis 50:3 *There was a period of national mourning for seventy days.*
Grief is a process that must not be denied or hurried. The rituals of wakes, visitations, funerals, and memorial services all help you move through the stages of grief.

Job 1:20-22 *Job stood up and tore his robe in grief. . . . He said ". . . The Lord gave me everything I had, and the Lord has taken it away."*
Losses always bring pain. Recognizing and expressing that pain is not wrong or sinful, but is rather a healthy expression of how God created us.

Lamentations 3:19-23 *The thought of my suffering and homelessness is bitter beyond words. I will never forget this awful time, as I grieve over my loss. Yet I still dare to hope when I remember this: The unfailing love of the Lord never ends! By his mercies we have been kept from complete destruction. Great is his faithfulness; his mercies begin afresh each day.*

Believers grieve with God, the source of greatest hope. Unbelievers grieve without God and therefore have no hope.

Hebrews 10:34 *You suffered along with those who were thrown into jail. When all you owned was taken from you, you accepted it with joy. You knew you had better things waiting for you in eternity.*
It is important to grieve, but recognize that grieving is short-term. One day you will be with God in heaven where all grief will be gone forever.

PROMISE FROM GOD
Psalm 56:8 *You keep track of all my sorrows. You have collected all my tears in your bottle. You have recorded each one in your book.*

Love of God

How can I know God really loves me?
John 3:16 *For God so loved the world that he gave his only Son, so that everyone who believes in him will not perish but have eternal life.*

1 John 4:9-10 *God showed how much he loved us by sending his only Son into the world so that we might have eternal life through him. This is real love.*
The gift of God's Son, Jesus Christ, is the ultimate expression of his love for you. Though he gives many other blessings, he can give no greater gift.

Romans 5:5 *[God] has given us the Holy Spirit to fill our hearts with his love.*

The gift of the Holy Spirit is also an assurance of God's love. Though it may be difficult to prove objectively, the Spirit gives you solid assurance of God's great love.

Romans 8:38 *Nothing can ever separate us from his love.*

God promises that nothing can come between his love and you. Nothing!

PROMISE FROM GOD

Psalm 23:6 *Surely your goodness and unfailing love will pursue me all the days of my life, and I will live in the house of the Lord forever.*

Meaning/Meaningless

What brings meaning to my life? What will make my life count?

Romans 11:36 *For everything comes from him; everything exists by his power and is intended for his glory. To him be glory evermore.*

Genesis 1:26 *Then God said, "Let us make people in our image, to be like ourselves."*

Isaiah 43:7 *All who claim me as their God will come, for I have made them for my glory. It was I who created them.*

God, as your Creator, gives you value. You are made in his image, and his very breath keeps you alive.

Ephesians 1:5 *His unchanging plan has always been to adopt us into his own family by bringing us to himself through Jesus Christ. And this gave him great pleasure.*

God's purpose for you is to be his child and to live in the complete security of his love every moment.

Romans 8:29 *For God knew his people in advance, and he chose them to become like his Son, so that his Son would be the firstborn, with many brothers and sisters.*

2 Peter 1:3 *As we know Jesus better, his divine power gives us everything we need for living a godly life. He has called us to receive his own glory and goodness!*

God intends for you to become more and more like the Lord Jesus.

Matthew 4:19 *Jesus called out to them, "Come, be my disciples, and I will show you how to fish for people!"*

Acts 20:24 *But my life is worth nothing unless I use it for doing the work assigned me by the Lord Jesus—the work of telling others the Good News about God's wonderful kindness and love.*

2 Corinthians 3:2 *But the only letter of recommendation we need is you yourselves! Your lives are a letter written in our hearts, and everyone can read it and recognize our good work among you.*

2 Corinthians 5:18 *All this newness of life is from God, who brought us back to himself through what Christ did. And God has given us the task of reconciling people to him.*
You have been called to participate in God's work in the world and make an eternal impact on others for him.

2 Corinthians 5:9 *So our aim is to please him always, whether we are here in this body or away from this body.*

1 Thessalonians 2:4 *For we speak as messengers who have been approved by God to be entrusted with the Good News. Our purpose is to please God, not people. He is the one who examines the motives of our hearts.*

Ecclesiastes 12:13 *Here is my final conclusion: Fear God and obey his commands, for this is the duty of every person.*

2 Timothy 2:21 *If you keep yourself pure, you will be a utensil God can use for his purpose. Your life will be clean, and you will be ready for the Master to use you for every good work.*
Pleasing God by obeying him and doing his will

prepares you to be used by God to accomplish his purposes for your life.

PROMISES FROM GOD

Philippians 1:9-10 *I pray that your love for each other will overflow more and more, and that you will keep on growing in your knowledge and understanding. For I want you to understand what really matters, so that you may live pure and blameless lives until Christ returns.*

Philippians 3:7-8 *I once thought all these things were so very important, but now I consider them worthless because of what Christ has done. Yes, everything else is worthless when compared with the priceless gain of knowing Christ Jesus my Lord. I have discarded everything else, counting it all as garbage, so that I may have Christ.*

Meditation

(*see also* Prayer)

To whom should my meditation be directed?

Psalm 63:6 *I lie awake thinking of you, meditating on you through the night.*

Psalm 48:9 *O God, we meditate on your unfailing love as we worship in your Temple.*

Psalm 145:5 *I will meditate on your majestic, glorious splendor and your wonderful miracles.*
Your moments of meditation should be about God and to God.

How do I meditate? What is involved in meditation?

Psalm 62:1, 5 *I wait quietly before God, for my salvation comes from him. . . . I wait quietly before God, for my hope is in him.*
Meditation is waiting quietly and patiently before God, putting your hope in him.

Psalm 1:2 *But they delight in doing everything the Lord wants; day and night they think about his law.*
Meditation is thinking about God's Word and what God tells you through his Word.

Psalm 16:7 *I will bless the Lord who guides me; even at night my heart instructs me.*
Meditation is a time of seeking God's guidance and instruction.

Psalm 143:5 *I remember the days of old. I ponder all your great works. I think about what you have done.*
Meditation is a time of reflection on God's past blessings.

PROMISE FROM GOD
2 Timothy 2:7 *Think about what I am saying. The Lord will give you understanding in all these things.*

Mercy

(*see also* Forgiveness, Grace)

What is mercy?

Psalm 103:8-10 *The Lord is merciful and gracious; he is slow to get angry and full of unfailing love. He will not constantly accuse us, nor remain angry forever. He has not punished us for all our sins, nor does he deal with us as we deserve.*

Lamentations 3:22 *The unfailing love of the Lord never ends! By his mercies we have been kept from complete destruction.*

Isaiah 63:9 *In all their suffering he also suffered, and he personally rescued them. In his love and mercy he redeemed them. He lifted them up and carried them through all the years.*

Micah 7:18 *Where is another God like you, who pardons the sins of the survivors among his people? You cannot stay angry with your people forever, because you delight in showing mercy.*

1 Peter 1:3 *All honor to the God and Father of our Lord Jesus Christ, for it is by his boundless mercy that God has given us the privilege of being born again.* Mercy is not receiving the punishment you should receive for your sins. It is receiving a beautiful gift (like salvation) that you don't deserve. Mercy is having favor with Almighty God. By his mercy,

God forgives your sins and gives you the opportunity to receive eternal life if you simply believe in him.

To whom does God show mercy?

Matthew 5:7 *God blesses those who are merciful, for they will be shown mercy.*
To the merciful.

Psalm 119:132 *Come and show me your mercy, as you do for all who love your name.*

Psalm 103:11 *For his unfailing love toward those who fear him is as great as the height of the heavens above the earth.*
To those who love, fear, and honor him.

Acts 2:21 *And anyone who calls on the name of the Lord will be saved.*
To those who ask.

Deuteronomy 13:18 *The Lord your God will be merciful only if you obey him and keep all the commands I am giving you today.*
To those with sincere hearts.

Exodus 33:19 *I will show kindness to anyone I choose.*

Romans 9:15-16 *For God said to Moses, "I will show mercy to anyone I choose, and I will show compassion to anyone I choose." So receiving God's promise is not up to us. We can't get it by choosing it or working hard for it. God will show mercy to anyone he chooses.*

Ultimately, God chooses who will receive his mercy. We cannot earn it. We are, literally, at his mercy.

How can I show mercy?

Colossians 3:12-13 *Since God chose you to be the holy people whom he loves, you must clothe yourselves with tenderhearted mercy, kindness, humility, gentleness, and patience. You must make allowance for each other's faults and forgive the person who offends you. Remember, the Lord forgave you, so you must forgive others.*

Forgive others.

Matthew 18:33 *Shouldn't you have mercy on your fellow servant, just as I had mercy on you?*

Share the mercy God has given you.

Micah 6:8 *No, O people, the Lord has already told you what is good, and this is what he requires: to do what is right, to love mercy, and to walk humbly with your God.*

Show mercy as an act of obedience to God.

Zechariah 7:9 *This is what the Lord Almighty says: Judge fairly and honestly, and show mercy and kindness to one another.*

Show mercy in judging fairly and honestly, and in showing kindness to others.

PROMISES FROM GOD

Hebrews 4:16   *So let us come boldly to the throne of our gracious God. There we will receive his mercy, and we will find grace to help us when we need it.*

2 Corinthians 1:3   *All praise to the God and Father of our Lord Jesus Christ. He is the source of every mercy and the God who comforts us.*

Miracles

(*see also* Healing)

How does God use miracles?

2 Kings 17:36   *Worship only the Lord, who brought you out of Egypt with such mighty miracles and power. You must worship him and bow before him; offer sacrifices to him alone.*

Daniel 6:27   *He rescues and saves his people; he performs miraculous signs and wonders in the heavens and on earth. He has rescued Daniel from the power of the lions.*

Micah 7:15   *"Yes," says the Lord, "I will do mighty miracles for you, like those I did when I rescued you from slavery in Egypt."*
God uses miracles to rescue us.

Exodus 10:1   *Then the Lord said to Moses, "Return to Pharaoh and again make your demands. I have made him and his officials stubborn so I can*

continue to display my power by performing miraculous signs among them."
God uses miracles to show his power.

Matthew 14:14 *A vast crowd was there as he stepped from the boat, and he had compassion on them and healed their sick.*
God uses miracles to show his love and compassion for us.

Should I be disappointed with God when he doesn't perform a miracle I pray for?

Psalm 107:1 *Give thanks to the Lord, for he is good! His faithful love endures forever.*
We don't know that God will always do miracles, but we do know that God's love for us is eternal and unchanging. You can therefore trust that God is doing a good work in your life even when he doesn't give you exactly what you pray for.

PROMISE FROM GOD
Luke 1:37 *For nothing is impossible with God.*

Mistakes

(*see also* Failure)

Is there hope for me, even with all the mistakes I've made?

Judges 16:17, 21, 28 *Finally, Samson told her his secret. . . . So the Philistines captured him and*

gouged out his eyes. . . . Then Samson prayed to the Lord, "Sovereign Lord, remember me again."
Samson's life, although filled with foolish mistakes, was still mightily used by God. If God refused to use his people when they made mistakes, he would never use his people.

J o n a h   1 : 3   *But Jonah got up and went in the opposite direction in order to get away from the Lord.*
The worst mistake you can make is running from God, yet God pursued Jonah and gave him another chance.

E x o d u s   2 : 1 2   *After looking around to make sure no one was watching, Moses killed the Egyptian and buried him in the sand.*
Even Moses' life was marred by an immature and terrible mistake.

2   C h r o n i c l e s   1 8 : 3 1 - 3 2   *So when the Aramean charioteers saw Jehoshaphat in his royal robes, they went after him. "There is the king of Israel!" they shouted. But Jehoshaphat cried out to the Lord to save him, and God helped him by turning the attack away from him. As soon as the charioteers realized he was not the king of Israel, they stopped chasing him.*
God still helped Jehoshaphat even though he made the mistake of ignoring Micaiah. God still helps you in the midst of your mistakes.

M a t t h e w   2 6 : 7 4   *Peter said, "I swear by God, I don't know the man."*

Jesus restored Peter to fellowship even after his most painful mistake. Following Christ means allowing him to forgive your mistakes and call you to a more glorious future.

Luke 1:18 *Zechariah said to the angel, "How can I know this will happen? I'm an old man now, and my wife is also well along in years."*
God did not disqualify Zechariah just because he had doubts.

When I make big mistakes, how do I move on?

Genesis 4:6-7 *"Why are you so angry?" the Lord asked him. "Why do you look so dejected? You will be accepted if you respond in the right way. But if you refuse to respond correctly, then watch out! Sin is waiting to attack and destroy you, and you must subdue it."*

2 Samuel 12:13 *Then David confessed to Nathan, "I have sinned against the Lord." Nathan replied, "Yes, but the Lord has forgiven you, and you won't die for this sin."*

1 John 1:10 *If we claim we have not sinned, we are calling God a liar and showing that his word has no place in our hearts.*

Proverbs 28:13 *People who cover over their sins will not prosper. But if they confess and forsake them, they will receive mercy.*

1 John 1:9 *But if we confess our sins to him, he is faithful and just to forgive us and to cleanse us from every wrong.*
Admit mistakes and sins to open the door to forgiveness and restoration of relationships.

1 Corinthians 10:1, 11 *I don't want you to forget, dear brothers and sisters, what happened to our ancestors in the wilderness long ago. . . . All these events happened to them as examples for us. They were written down to warn us, who live at the time when this age is drawing to a close.*
If you don't learn from others' and your own past mistakes, you will be lulled into a sense of false security. Learning from past mistakes prepares you to not repeat them in the future.

Jeremiah 8:4-5 *Jeremiah, say to the people, "This is what the Lord says: When people fall down, don't they get up again? When they start down the wrong road and discover their mistake, don't they turn back? Then why do these people keep going along their self-destructive path, refusing to turn back, even though I have warned them?"*

Hebrews 12:1 *Therefore, since we are surrounded by such a huge crowd of witnesses to the life of faith, let us strip off every weight that slows us down, especially the sin that so easily hinders our progress. And let us run with endurance the race that God has set before us.*

Focus forward! Once forgiven, don't linger. The future is ahead, not behind.

PROMISE FROM GOD

Philippians 3:12-14 *I don't mean to say that I have already achieved these things or that I have already reached perfection! But I keep working toward that day when I will finally be all that Christ Jesus saved me for and wants me to be. No, dear brothers and sisters, I am still not all I should be, but I am focusing all my energies on this one thing: Forgetting the past and looking forward to what lies ahead, I strain to reach the end of the race and receive the prize for which God, through Christ Jesus, is calling us up to heaven.*

Misunderstandings

How should I respond to misunderstandings?

1 Corinthians 12:1 *And now, dear brothers and sisters, I will write about the special abilities the Holy Spirit gives to each of us, for I must correct your misunderstandings about them.*

Luke 19:11 *The crowd was listening to everything Jesus said. And because he was nearing Jerusalem, he told a story to correct the impression that the Kingdom of God would begin right away.*

Joshua 22:10-13 *But while they were still in Canaan, before they crossed the Jordan River, Reuben, Gad, and the half-tribe of Manasseh built a very large altar near the Jordan River at a place called Geliloth. When the rest of Israel heard they had built the altar at Geliloth west of the Jordan River, in the land of Canaan, the whole assembly gathered at Shiloh and prepared to go to war against their brother tribes. First, however, they sent a delegation led by Phinehas son of Eleazar, the priest. They crossed the river to talk with the tribes of Reuben, Gad, and the half-tribe of Manasseh*

You should have a desire to correct misunderstandings and proactively resolve them. Uncorrected, misunderstandings can lead to very undesirable outcomes.

Joshua 22:16, 21-23, 29 *"The whole community of the Lord demands to know why you are betraying the God of Israel. How could you turn away from the Lord and build an altar in rebellion against him?" . . . Then the people of Reuben, Gad, and the half-tribe of Manasseh answered these high officials: "The Lord alone is God! The Lord alone is God! We have not built the altar in rebellion against the Lord. If we have done so, do not spare our lives this day. But the Lord knows, and let all Israel know, too, that we have not built an altar for ourselves to turn away from the Lord. Nor will we use it for our burnt offerings or grain offerings or peace offerings. If we have built it for this purpose, may the Lord himself punish us. . . . Far be it from us to rebel against the Lord or turn away from him by building our own altar for burnt offerings, grain offerings, or sacrifices. Only the altar of the Lord our God that stands in front of the Tabernacle may be used for that purpose."*

If you desire to communicate openly, both parties speak and listen so as to fully ascertain and understand the facts. This will help resolve and avoid misunderstandings.

PROMISES FROM GOD

1 Corinthians 13:12 *Now we see things imperfectly as in a poor mirror, but then we will see everything with perfect clarity. All that I know now is partial and incomplete, but then I will know everything completely, just as God knows me now.*

Philippians 3:15 *I hope all of you who are mature Christians will agree on these things. If you disagree on some point, I believe God will make it plain to you.*

Neglect

(*see also* Abandonment, Loneliness)

What can I do when I feel neglected?

Psalm 66:20 *Praise God, who did not ignore my prayer and did not withdraw his unfailing love from me.*

While others may neglect you, God never turns away from us.

Psalm 68:4 *Rejoice in his presence!*

James 4:8 *Draw close to God, and God will draw close to you.*

When you feel neglected, you must not let these feelings cause you to withdraw from God. Draw near to God. His presence will give you the joy you need.

PROMISE FROM GOD
Hebrews 12:15 *Look after each other so that none of you will miss out on the special favor of God. Watch out that no bitter root of unbelief rises up among you, for whenever it springs up, many are corrupted by its poison.*

Oppression

(*see also* Persecution, Spiritual Warfare, Suffering)

What does God think of oppression?

Zechariah 7:10 *Do not oppress widows, orphans, foreigners, and poor people.*

God hates oppression and expressly forbids it in any form.

Does God care about oppressed people?

Psalm 72:12 *He will help the oppressed, who have no one to defend them.*

God has a special love for those who are oppressed and he promises to be with them and help them.

Zephaniah 3:19 *And I will deal severely with all who have oppressed you.*

God promises to judge oppressors.

Luke 4:18-19 *The Spirit of the Lord is upon me, for he has appointed me to preach Good News to the poor. He has sent me to proclaim that captives will be released, that the blind will see, that the downtrodden will be freed from their oppressors, and that the time of the Lord's favor has come.*

Freeing the oppressed was a central component of Jesus' earthly ministry.

What does God call us to do about oppression?

Amos 5:23-24 *Away with your hymns of praise! They are only noise to my ears. I will not listen to your music, no matter how lovely it is. Instead, I want to see a mighty flood of justice, a river of righteous living that will never run dry.*

God urges us to recognize that doing justice is central to godly living. Wonderful worship and pious prayer are exposed as hypocrisy if they are not accompanied by opposing oppression and aiding the oppressed.

Ezekiel 45:9 *For this is what the Sovereign Lord says: Enough, you princes of Israel! Stop all your violence and oppression and do what is just and right.*

Refuse to participate in any form of oppression. Be willing, in whatever way you can, to call those in power to account.

Psalm 72:1, 4 *Give justice to the king, O God, and righteousness to the king's son. . . . Help him to defend the poor, to rescue the children of the needy, and to crush their oppressors.*
Pray that your leaders will protect the weak and punish any who oppress them. Pray for the leaders of other countries to be fair and just, and to refuse to oppress any of their people.

PROMISE FROM GOD
Psalm 9:9 *The Lord is a shelter for the oppressed, a refuge in times of trouble.*

Overcoming

(*see also* Perseverance, Persistence, Victory)

Can I overcome the disadvantages of my birth and the dysfunction of my family of origin?

Judges 11:1-2 *Now Jephthah of Gilead was a great warrior. He was the son of Gilead, but his mother was a prostitute. Gilead's wife also had several sons, and when these half brothers grew up, they chased Jephthah off the land. "You will not get any of our father's inheritance," they said, "for you are the son of a prostitute."*

Despite being scorned and rejected because of his illegitimate birth, Jephthah became a military hero and judge of all Israel.

2 Kings 11:1-3 *When Athaliah, the mother of King Ahaziah of Judah, learned that her son was dead, she set out to destroy the rest of the royal family. But Ahaziah's sister Jehosheba, the daughter of King Jehoram, took Ahaziah's infant son, Joash, and stole him away from among the rest of the king's children, who were about to be killed. Jehosheba put Joash and his nurse in a bedroom to hide him from Athaliah, so the child was not murdered. Joash and his nurse remained hidden in the Temple of the Lord for six years while Athaliah ruled the land.*

Joash was raised in hiding after the rest of his family was murdered, yet he became one of the wisest and most godly kings of Judah.

Genesis 41:41 *And Pharaoh said to Joseph, "I hereby put you in charge of the entire land of Egypt."* Joseph's brothers hated him so much that they sold him as a slave. Yet Joseph trusted God and maintained his own integrity, and he became a wise and powerful ruler.

How can I be an overcomer?

Psalm 116:3-5 *Death had its hands around my throat; the terrors of the grave overtook me. I saw only* trouble and sorrow. Then I called on the name of the Lord: "Please, Lord, save me!" How kind the Lord is! How good he is! So merciful, this God of ours!

Prayer is essential to winning the victory.

2 Corinthians 4:8-9 *We are pressed on every side by troubles, but we are not crushed and broken. We are perplexed, but we don't give up and quit. We are hunted down, but God never abandons us. We get knocked down, but we get up again and keep going.*

Philippians 4:13 *For I can do everything with the help of Christ who gives me the strength I need.*

With confidence in God's presence, you must develop the ability to endure setbacks without surrendering.

2 Corinthians 4:18 *So we don't look at the troubles we can see right now; rather, we look forward to what we have not yet seen. For the troubles we see will soon be over, but the joys to come will last forever.*

An eternal perspective is an indispensable attribute of the overcomer. Unseen solutions will replace visible problems.

PROMISES FROM GOD

Job 17:9 *The righteous will move onward and forward, and those with pure hearts will become stronger and stronger.*

John 16:33 *I have told you all this so that you may have peace in me. Here on earth you will have*

many trials and sorrows. But take heart, because
I have overcome the world.

Overwhelmed

How does God help me when I am overwhelmed?

Romans 8:38-39 *Nothing can ever separate us from his love. Death can't, and life can't. The angels can't, and the demons can't. Our fears for today, our worries about tomorrow, and even the powers of hell can't keep God's love away. Whether we are high above the sky or in the deepest ocean, nothing in all creation will ever be able to separate us from the love of God that is revealed in Christ Jesus our Lord.*
God's love is certain, consistent, ever present, and victorious.

Psalm 46:1-2 *God is our refuge and strength, always ready to help in times of trouble. So we will not fear, even if earthquakes come and the mountains crumble into the sea.*

John 14:27 *I am leaving you with a gift—peace of mind and heart. And the peace I give isn't like the peace the world gives. So don't be troubled or afraid.*
God's presence gives you peace of mind and heart in overwhelming situations.

Psalm 119:92-93 *If your law hadn't sustained me with joy, I would have died in my misery. I will never forget your commandments, for you have used them to restore my joy and health.*

Psalm 119:143 *As pressure and stress bear down on me, I find joy in your commands.*
God's Word brings deep joy and contentment in the midst of overwhelming circumstances.

Psalm 142:1-3 *I cry out to the Lord; I plead for the Lord's mercy. I pour out my complaints before him and tell him all my troubles. For I am overwhelmed, and you alone know the way I should turn.*
Prayer—honestly talking and listening to God— keeps you in touch with the One whose help you need most.

Matthew 11:28-29 *Then Jesus said, "Come to me, all of you who are weary and carry heavy burdens, and I will give you rest. Take my yoke upon you. Let me teach you, because I am humble and gentle, and you will find rest for your souls."*
A healthy, growing, daily relationship with God puts overwhelming circumstances in perspective.

2 Corinthians 1:8-10 *I think you ought to know, dear brothers and sisters, about the trouble we went through in the province of Asia. We were crushed and completely overwhelmed, and we thought we would never live through it. In fact, we expected to die. But as a result, we learned not to rely on ourselves, but on God who can raise the*

*dead. And he did deliver us from mortal danger.
And we are confident that he will continue to
deliver us.*

When your troubles are overwhelming, continue
to look to God and his power to help you.
Bravely keep your focus on God and patiently
watch him work.

How do I keep perspective when I'm over-whelmed?

Psalm 3:1-2   *O Lord, I have so many enemies;
so many are against me. So many are saying, "God
will never rescue him!"*

Psalm 116:3-4   *Death had its hands around my
throat; the terrors of the grave overtook me. I saw only
trouble and sorrow. Then I called on the name of the
Lord: "Please, Lord, save me!"*

Stop listening to the onslaught of voices around
you and focus on listening to God.

Deuteronomy 20:1   *When you go out to fight
your enemies and you face horses and chariots and an
army greater than your own, do not be afraid. The
Lord your God, who brought you safely out of Egypt, is
with you!*

Psalm 27:14   *Wait patiently for the Lord. Be
brave and courageous. Yes, wait patiently for the
Lord.*

Recognize the issues, overwhelming as they may
be. But don't stop there! Recognize who God is

and take courage. Expectantly look to him
for help.

2 Corinthians 4:8-10 *We are pressed on
every side by troubles, but we are not crushed and
broken. We are perplexed, but we don't give up and
quit. We are hunted down, but God never abandons
us. We get knocked down, but we get up again and
keep going. Through suffering, these bodies of ours
constantly share in the death of Jesus so that the life
of Jesus may also be seen in our bodies.*
God will never abandon you. Look at your overwhelming situation from his perspective. Watch
how he is transforming you into the likeness of
Jesus.

PROMISE FROM GOD
Psalm 71:15 *I will tell everyone about your
righteousness. All day long I will proclaim your saving
power, for I am overwhelmed by how much you have
done for me.*

$\mathcal{P}ain$

(*see also* Grief, Suffering)

What will heal my pain?
Psalm 25:17-18 *My problems go from bad to
worse. Oh, save me from them all! Feel my pain and
see my trouble. Forgive all my sins.*

Acknowledge your pain honestly to God in prayer. Start by calling to him for help. This is where you must begin the process of healing.

John 9:2-3 *"Teacher," his disciples asked him, "why was this man born blind? Was it a result of his own sins or those of his parents?" "It was not because of his sins or his parents' sins," Jesus answered. "He was born blind so the power of God could be seen in him."*

1 Samuel 5:6-7 *Then the Lord began to afflict the people of Ashdod and the nearby villages with a plague of tumors. When the people realized what was happening, they cried out, "We can't keep the Ark of the God of Israel here any longer! He is against us! We will all be destroyed along with our god Dagon."*

Psalm 139:23-24 *Search me, O God, and know my heart; test me and know my thoughts. Point out anything in me that offends you, and lead me along the path of everlasting life.*

Determine the source of your pain. It may or may not be a consequence of your own sin, or it may be someone else who has hurt you. As you seek God in prayer and talk with others (family, close friends, trained counselors), the source of your pain will become clear. Only then can you develop the right plan for dealing with it.

Psalm 119:28, 50, 52, 92 *I weep with grief; encourage me by your word. . . . Your promise*

revives me; it comforts me in all my troubles. . . .
I meditate on your age-old laws; O Lord, they comfort
me. . . . If your law hadn't sustained me with joy,
I would have died in my misery.

Immerse yourself in God's Word and find
encouragement, revival, comfort, joy, and insight.

1 Peter 4:1-2 *So then, since Christ suffered*
physical pain, you must arm yourselves with the same
attitude he had, and be ready to suffer, too. For if you
are willing to suffer for Christ, you have decided to
stop sinning. And you won't spend the rest of your life
chasing after evil desires, but you will be anxious to
do the will of God.

Develop a godly perspective toward pain. This
helps you focus less on the pain itself (which can
cause bitterness and discouragement) and more
on how this pain can help you develop stronger
character.

Colossians 3:16 *Let the words of Christ, in all*
their richness, live in your hearts and make you wise.
Use his words to teach and counsel each other. Sing
psalms and hymns and spiritual songs to God with
thankful hearts.

Psalm 37:30-31 *The godly offer good counsel;*
they know what is right from wrong. They fill their
hearts with God's law, so they will never slip from his
path.

Proverbs 27:9 *The heartfelt counsel of a friend*
is as sweet as perfume and incense.

Seek help from godly counselors. Sometimes it is enough to seek advice from trusted friends and family. At other times it is necessary to talk with a trained counselor who can help you pinpoint your pain and provide effective ways, in accordance with God's Word, to deal with it.

Revelation 21:1-4 *Then I saw a new heaven and a new earth, for the old heaven and the old earth had disappeared. . . . I heard a loud shout from the throne, saying, "Look, the home of God is now among his people! He will live with them, and they will be his people. God himself will be with them. He will remove all of their sorrows, and there will be no more death or sorrow or crying or pain. For the old world and its evils are gone forever."*
Recognize that pain will not go on forever. In heaven, there will be no more pain.

Colossians 3:13 *You must make allowance for each other's faults and forgive the person who offends you. Remember, the Lord forgave you, so you must forgive others.*
Forgiving those who have sinned against you does wonders in removing the pain of hurt, anger, and bitterness in your heart.

1 Peter 3:9 *Don't repay evil for evil. Don't retaliate when people say unkind things about you. Instead, pay them back with a blessing. That is what God wants you to do, and he will bless you for it.*

Bless those who cause you pain, for retaliation and revenge compound pain.

2 Samuel 18:33 *The king was overcome with emotion. He went up to his room over the gateway and burst into tears. And as he went, he cried, "O my son Absalom! My son, my son Absalom! If only I could have died instead of you! O Absalom, my son, my son."*

Ecclesiastes 3:4 *A time to cry and a time to laugh. A time to grieve and a time to dance.* Express your pain and don't cover it, for expression brings relief.

2 Corinthians 2:5 *I am not overstating it when I say that the man who caused all the trouble hurt your entire church more than he hurt me.*

Philippians 2:4 *Don't think only about your own affairs, but be interested in others, too, and what they are doing.* Realize others may be hurting, too. Be sensitive to them and their pain, taking the focus off of yourself.

How is pain good for me? What can I learn from it?

2 Corinthians 7:8-10 *I am no longer sorry that I sent that letter to you, though I was sorry for a time, for I know that it was painful to you for a little while. Now I am glad I sent it, not because it hurt* *you, but because the pain caused you to have remorse and change your ways. . . . For God can use sorrow in our lives to help us turn away from sin and seek salvation.*

Pain can be redemptive. Your broken heart can lead you to God through the realization, confession, and repentance of sin.

1 Peter 4:19 *So if you are suffering according to God's will, keep on doing what is right, and trust yourself to the God who made you, for he will never fail you.*

Pain can bring you closer to God.

John 11:14-15 *Then he told them plainly, "Lazarus is dead. And for your sake, I am glad I wasn't there, because this will give you another opportunity to believe in me. Come, let's go see him."*

Pain can reveal God's power.

Hebrews 12:11 *No discipline is enjoyable while it is happening—it is painful! But afterward there will be a quiet harvest of right living for those who are trained in this way.*

Painful discipline can help you make right choices in the future.

Job 6:10 *At least I can take comfort in this: Despite the pain, I have not denied the words of the Holy One.*

Pain can test and prove your commitment to God.

Romans 5:3-4 *We can rejoice, too, when we run into problems and trials, for we know that they are good for us—they help us learn to endure. And endurance develops strength of character in us, and character strengthens our confident expectation of salvation.*

Pain can strengthen your character.

2 Corinthians 1:4, 6 *He comforts us in all our troubles so that we can comfort others. When others are troubled, we will be able to give them the same comfort God has given us. . . . So when we are weighed down with troubles, it is for your benefit and salvation! For when God comforts us, it is so that we, in turn, can be an encouragement to you. Then you can patiently endure the same things we suffer.*

Pain equips you to comfort others.

Romans 8:18 *Yet what we suffer now is nothing compared to the glory he will give us later.*

Pain sparks the anticipation of the return of Jesus and your eternal life in heaven with him.

PROMISE FROM GOD

Revelation 21:4 *He will remove all of their sorrows, and there will be no more death or sorrow or crying or pain. For the old world and its evils are gone forever.*

Panic

What happens to me when I panic?

Psalm 22:14 *My life is poured out like water, and all my bones are out of joint. My heart is like wax, melting within me.*

Panic has emotional, mental, and physical effects.

Daniel 2:10-11 *The astrologers replied to the king, "There isn't a man alive who can tell Your Majesty his dream! And no king, however great and powerful, has ever asked such a thing of any magician, enchanter, or astrologer! This is an impossible thing the king requires. No one except the gods can tell you your dream, and they do not live among people."*

Panic feeds feelings of hopelessness. When your security fades, hope fades too.

Matthew 14:30 *But when he looked around at the high waves, he was terrified and began to sink. "Save me, Lord!" he shouted.*

Fear, the companion of panic, takes your focus off of who God is and what he can do.

2 Chronicles 20:22-23 *At the moment they began to sing and give praise, the Lord caused the armies of Ammon, Moab, and Mount Seir to start fighting among themselves. The armies of Moab and Ammon turned against their allies from Mount Seir and killed every one of them. After they had finished off the army of Seir, they turned on each other.*

Panic can be self-destructive, causing you to lash out at those around you.

2 Samuel 17:9-10 *He has probably already hidden in some pit or cave. And when he comes out and attacks and a few of your men fall, there will be panic among your troops, and everyone will start shouting that your men are being slaughtered. Then even the bravest of them, though they have the heart of a lion, will be paralyzed with fear. For all Israel knows what a mighty man your father is and how courageous his warriors are.*

Panic can be debilitating, robbing you of your vitality.

1 Samuel 13:6 *When the men of Israel saw the vast number of enemy troops, they lost their nerve entirely and tried to hide in caves, holes, rocks, tombs, and cisterns.*

Panic breeds cowardliness. When you lose courage you want to run.

Deuteronomy 20:8 *Then the officers will also say, "Is anyone terrified? If you are, go home before you frighten anyone else."*

Panic spreads easily and quickly.

How should I deal with panic? How do I find peace and perspective in the midst of panic?

Philippians 4:6-7 *Don't worry about anything; instead, pray about everything. Tell God* *what you need, and thank him for all he has done. If you do this, you will experience God's peace, which is far more wonderful than the human mind can understand. His peace will guard your hearts and minds as you live in Christ Jesus.*

Don't worry; pray. Worry mires you down in what you can't do. Prayer lifts you up to realize what God can do.

2 Chronicles 20:3 *Jehoshaphat was alarmed by this news and sought the Lord for guidance. He also gave orders that everyone throughout Judah should observe a fast.*

James 1:5 *If you need wisdom—if you want to know what God wants you to do—ask him, and he will gladly tell you. He will not resent your asking.* Seek the Lord's guidance in faith. Since God knows everything, it makes good sense that he knows what you should do next.

Psalm 119:95, 103-105, 165 *Though the wicked hide along the way to kill me, I will quietly keep my mind on your decrees. . . . How sweet are your words to my taste; they are sweeter than honey. Your commandments give me understanding; no wonder I hate every false way of life. Your word is a lamp for my feet and a light for my path. . . . Those who love your law have great peace and do not stumble.*

Go to God's Word. Take comfort in his promises; seek his perspective; relax in his peace.

Psalm 63:8 *I follow close behind you; your strong right hand holds me securely.*
Listen to God and follow his way. When you are certain you are following God's way, you will be calm and confident.

Psalm 112:7 *They do not fear bad news; they confidently trust the Lord to care for them.*

Daniel 2:12-14 *The king was furious when he heard this, and he sent out orders to execute all the wise men of Babylon. And because of the king's decree, men were sent to find and kill Daniel and his friends. When Arioch, the commander of the king's guard, came to kill them, Daniel handled the situation with wisdom and discretion.*
Act deliberately with wisdom and discretion. Understand God's perspective on life and have full confidence in him.

Isaiah 26:3 *You will keep in perfect peace all who trust in you, whose thoughts are fixed on you!*

1 Thessalonians 5:8 *But let us who live in the light think clearly, protected by the body armor of faith and love, and wearing as our helmet the confidence of our salvation.*
Focus your thoughts clearly on God. Make sure that he is part of each solution you are considering.

Psalm 3:5-6 *I lay down and slept. I woke up in safety, for the Lord was watching over me. I am not*

afraid of ten thousand enemies who surround me
on every side.

Literally, rest in the Lord. When you realize God
is in control you can sleep tonight.

Psalm 46:10 *Be silent, and know that I am
God! I will be honored by every nation. I will be
honored throughout the world.*

Proverbs 19:23 *Fear of the Lord gives life,
security, and protection from harm.*

Isaiah 8:13 *Do not fear anything except the
Lord Almighty. He alone is the Holy One. If you fear
him, you need fear nothing else.*

Really get to know God. To know what God
says is important. To know his will is more
important. But to know God personally is most
important.

PROMISES FROM GOD

Psalm 75:3 *When the earth quakes and its
people live in turmoil, I am the one who keeps its
foundations firm.*

Isaiah 41:10 *Don't be afraid, for I am with
you. Do not be dismayed, for I am your God. I will
strengthen you. I will help you. I will uphold you with
my victorious right hand.*

Past

(*see also* Regrets)

How can I most effectively deal with a hurtful past?

Genesis 50:19-20 *But Joseph told them, "Don't be afraid of me. Am I God, to judge and punish you? As far as I am concerned, God turned into good what you meant for evil."*

Matthew 18:20-21 *Then Peter came to him and asked, "Lord, how often should I forgive someone who sins against me? Seven times?" "No!" Jesus replied, "seventy times seven!"*
Forgiving is essential to the healing process. As you release those who have hurt you, you are free to be healed and to grow beyond the pain.

Zechariah 8:13 *Among the nations, Judah and Israel had become symbols of what it means to be cursed. But no longer! Now I will rescue you and make you both a symbol and a source of blessing! So don't be afraid or discouraged, but instead get on with rebuilding the Temple!*

Genesis 41:51 *Joseph named his older son Manasseh, for he said, "God has made me forget all my troubles and the family of my father."*
When you dwell on the past, it is hard to forget it and move on. Deal with the pain of the past

so you can receive the blessings God wants to give you today. Then you can move forward toward a future of joy and healing.

How should I forgive those who have hurt me in the past?

Ephesians 4:32 *Instead, be kind to each other, tenderhearted, forgiving one another, just as God through Christ has forgiven you.*

Matthew 6:12 *Forgive us our sins, just as we have forgiven those who have sinned against us.*

Luke 6:37 *Stop judging others, and you will not be judged. Stop criticizing others, or it will all come back on you. If you forgive others, you will be forgiven.*

Forgive others as God has forgiven you, which is completely. God's forgiveness is not based on the goodness of the offender or the degree of the offense, but solely on his loving character. Forgiveness does not erase the offense, but pardons the offender. Forgiveness is a choice, a commitment to reflect God's love for you to others.

How do I deal with regrets?

Psalm 32:5 *Finally, I confessed all my sins to you and stopped trying to hide them. I said to myself, "I will confess my rebellion to the Lord." And you forgave me! All my guilt is gone.*

171

Ask for God's forgiveness. He has an endless supply, but you must ask for it.

Psalm 130:3-4 *Lord, if you kept a record of our sins, who, O Lord, could ever survive? But you offer forgiveness, that we might learn to fear you.*

Colossians 1:14 *God has purchased our freedom with his blood and has forgiven all our sins.* Receive God's forgiveness. Forgiveness isn't worth much until you accept it.

Psalm 32:1 *Oh, what joy for those whose rebellion is forgiven, whose sin is put out of sight!*

Isaiah 54:4 *Fear not; you will no longer live in shame. The shame of your youth and the sorrows of widowhood will be remembered no more.* Rejoice in being truly forgiven. Forgiveness is a time for celebration.

2 Corinthians 5:17 *What this means is that those who become Christians become new persons. They are not the same anymore, for the old life is gone. A new life has begun!* Regrets are like a dirty window that keeps you from seeing clearly what is in front of you. But God is in the cleaning business. He washes away the sins of the past as well as the guilt over those sins. If he forgets them completely, so can you. Choose to move forward joyfully, without carrying the burden of regret.

PROMISES FROM GOD
Hebrews 8:12 *And I will forgive their wrongdoings, and I will never again remember their sins.*

Patience

How can I develop more patience?

James 5:7 *Consider the farmers who eagerly look for the rains in the fall and in the spring. They patiently wait for the precious harvest to ripen.*

Habakkuk 2:3 *But these things I plan won't happen right away. Slowly, steadily, surely, the time approaches when the vision will be fulfilled. If it seems slow, wait patiently, for it will surely take place. It will not be delayed.*

Whether you're waiting for crops to ripen, a traffic jam to unsnarl, a child to mature, or God to perfect you, you can grow in patience by recognizing that these things take time and there is only so much you can do—if anything—to speed them up. A key to understanding God's will is to understand God's timing.

Romans 8:25 *But if we look forward to something we don't have yet, we must wait patiently and confidently.*

Patience is produced by the hope a believer has in God's eternal plan. When the long-range future is totally secure, you can be more patient with today's frustrations.

Where do I find the resources to be patient?

Galatians 5:22 *But when the Holy Spirit controls our lives, he will produce this kind of fruit in us: love, joy, peace, patience.*
A fruit of the Holy Spirit is patience. As you relax and trust in the Lord through the Holy Spirit, you release your need to control and manipulate people and life circumstances.

Colossians 1:11 *We also pray that you will be strengthened with his glorious power so that you will have all the patience and endurance you need. May you be filled with joy.*
Prayer, your own and others' prayers for you, help infuse patience into your life. When you admit your need through prayer, the Lord begins to meet that need.

Psalm 37:34 *Don't be impatient for the Lord to act! Travel steadily along his path. He will honor you, giving you the land. You will see the wicked destroyed.*
Patience also comes from simply trusting God day by day. Even when you don't think you can last for long, God gives you the strength to "travel steadily." Your commitments to faith and obedience will keep you on God's path for longer than you thought possible.

PROMISES FROM GOD

Isaiah 30:18   *But the Lord still waits for you to come to him so he can show you his love and compassion. For the Lord is a faithful God. Blessed are those who wait for him to help them.*

Isaiah 40:31   *But those who wait on the Lord will find new strength. They will fly high on wings like eagles. They will run and not grow weary. They will walk and not faint.*

Lamentations 3:25   *The Lord is wonderfully good to those who wait for him and seek him.*

Peace

How can I find peace within?

Isaiah 9:6-7   *For a child is born to us, a son is given to us. And the government will rest on his shoulders. These will be his royal titles: Wonderful Counselor, Mighty God, Everlasting Father, Prince of Peace. His ever expanding, peaceful government will never end. He will rule forever with fairness and justice from the throne of his ancestor David. The passionate commitment of the Lord Almighty will guarantee this!*

Psalm 29:11   *The Lord gives his people strength. The Lord blesses them with peace.*

Lasting peace comes only from Jesus Christ, the

Prince of Peace. His rule over all creation as well as in our lives ensures it. You find peace within when you let the Prince of Peace reign over your life.

Psalm 3:5 *I lay down and slept. I woke up in safety, for the Lord was watching over me.*

Psalm 4:8 *I will lie down in peace and sleep, for you alone, O Lord, will keep me safe.*
Inner peace comes from knowing that God is always watching over you. As the watchman kept guard over the city, so the Lord watches over you—day and night.

Philippians 4:6-7 *Don't worry about anything; instead, pray about everything. Tell God what you need, and thank him for all he has done. If you do this, you will experience God's peace, which is far more wonderful than the human mind can understand. His peace will guard your hearts and minds as you live in Christ Jesus.*
Prayer is a gateway to peace. Your spirits lighten as you unburden your soul to the Lord. His peace is like a guard on patrol, protecting you from any assaults of anxiety or concern.

Isaiah 26:3 *You will keep in perfect peace all who trust in you, whose thoughts are fixed on you!*
You find peace when you remove your eyes from your problems and rivet your attention on your Lord.

Psalm 119:165 *Those who love your law have great peace and do not stumble.*
Peace comes from knowing and living according to God's Word. His wisdom and direction guide you into the ways of life and lead you out of conflict, compromise, and deception.

John 14:27 *I am leaving you with a gift—peace of mind and heart. And the peace I give isn't like the peace the world gives. So don't be troubled or afraid.*

Galatians 5:22 *But when the Holy Spirit controls our lives, he will produce this kind of fruit in us: . . . peace.*
The Holy Spirit brings peace into your life.

How can I make peace with others?

2 Corinthians 13:11 *Rejoice. Change your ways. Encourage each other. Live in harmony and peace. Then the God of love and peace will be with you.*
Working hard at ridding sin from your own life while diligently building others up helps achieve peace.

Ephesians 4:3 *Always keep yourselves united in the Holy Spirit, and bind yourselves together with peace.*
Seek the unity that comes from the Holy Spirit.

Jeremiah 29:7 *And work for the peace and prosperity of Babylon.*

Matthew 5:9 *God blesses those who work for peace.*
Peace involves dealing with conflict appropriately. Peace is not always the absence of conflict. God calls us to pursue peace, which involves hard work.

Romans 12:17-18 *Never pay back evil for evil to anyone. . . . Do your part to live in peace with everyone.*
If you harbor feelings of revenge in your heart, you cannot be at peace with others.

James 3:17 *The wisdom that comes from heaven . . . is also peace loving, gentle at all times, and willing to yield to others. It is full of mercy and good deeds. It shows no partiality and is always sincere.*
Commit yourself to the good deeds that are the mark of a true peacemaker.

PROMISES FROM GOD

Psalm 34:14-15 *Turn away from evil and do good. Work hard at living in peace with others. The eyes of the Lord watch over those who do right; his ears are open to their cries for help.*

Psalm 37:37 *Look at those who are honest and good, for a wonderful future lies before those who love peace.*

Persecution

(*see also* Oppression, Spiritual Warfare, Suffering)

Where can I find hope when I am persecuted?

2 Timothy 3:12   *Yes, and everyone who wants to live a godly life in Christ Jesus will suffer persecution.*

1 Peter 4:13   *Instead, be very glad—because these trials will make you partners with Christ in his suffering, and afterward you will have the wonderful joy of sharing his glory.*

If you are being persecuted for your faith, you can be encouraged by the fact that many other faithful believers are also experiencing persecution. The Bible encourages you to see persecution for Jesus' sake as an honor. It is evidence of the depth of your commitment to Jesus and therefore a privilege to suffer for the God you love so much. It also acknowledges the depth of suffering Jesus went through for us.

Matthew 5:11   *God blesses you when you are mocked and persecuted and lied about because you are my followers.*

Jesus promises special blessings to those who are persecuted.

How should I respond when I am persecuted for my faith?

Psalm 69:1, 4   *Save me, O God. . . . Those who hate me without cause are more numerous than the hairs on my head.*

Turn to prayer in times of persecution. Only God can give you the strength to endure.

Luke 6:28   *Pray for the happiness of those who curse you.*

Matthew 5:44   *But I say, love your enemies! Pray for those who persecute you!*

Romans 12:14   *If people persecute you because you are a Christian, don't curse them; pray that God will bless them.*

Pray that God will bless those who persecute you, for it may be through your godly response to their persecution that God touches a hard heart and turns it to him.

Revelation 14:12   *Let this encourage God's holy people to endure persecution patiently and remain firm to the end, obeying his commands and trusting in Jesus.*

Remain obedient to God and endure the persecution patiently.

PROMISES FROM GOD

2 Corinthians 1:5   *You can be sure that the more we suffer for Christ, the more God will shower us with his comfort through Christ.*

Revelation 2:10 *Don't be afraid of what you are about to suffer. . . . Remain faithful even when facing death, and I will give you the crown of life.*

$\mathcal{P}erseverance$

(*see also* Endurance, Overcoming, Persistence, Victory)

How do I develop perseverance in my life?

Joshua 6:3 *Your entire army is to march around the city once a day for six days.*
Perseverance is obeying even when God's way doesn't seem to make sense or produce immediate results.

Nehemiah 6:12 *I realized that God had not spoken to him.*
The Christian's task and the perseverance to finish the task are rooted in God's call. If the work you do is God's work, you had better involve God in it. And if the work you do is God's work, you can have faith that your perseverance will pay off.

2 Corinthians 8:10-11 *I suggest that you finish what you started a year ago, for you were the first to propose this idea, and you were the first to begin doing something about it. Now you should carry this project through to completion just as enthusiastically as you began it.*

Perseverance involves setting manageable goals that keep you on track to finish what you started. If you don't set goals, you will never reach them.

PROMISES FROM GOD

Philippians 1:6 *And I am sure that God, who began the good work within you, will continue his work until it is finally finished on that day when Christ Jesus comes back again.*

Hebrews 3:14 *For if we are faithful to the end, trusting God just as firmly as when we first believed, we will share in all that belongs to Christ.*

Persistence

(*see also* Endurance, Overcoming, Perseverance)

How is persistence an important character quality?

Genesis 18:32 *Finally, Abraham said, "Lord, please do not get angry; I will speak but once more! Suppose only ten are found there?" And the Lord said, "Then, for the sake of the ten, I will not destroy it."* Persistence in prayer is vital for effective intercession.

Genesis 32:26-29 *The man said, "Let me go, for it is dawn." But Jacob panted, "I will not let you go unless you bless me." "What is your name?" the* man asked. He replied, "Jacob." "Your name will no longer be Jacob," the man told him. "It is now Israel, because you have struggled with both God and men and have won." . . . Then he blessed Jacob there.

Luke 11:8 *I tell you this—though he won't do it as a friend, if you keep knocking long enough, he will get up and give you what you want so his reputation won't be damaged.*

Luke 18:5 *This woman is driving me crazy. I'm going to see that she gets justice, because she is wearing me out with her constant requests!* Persistence is often the key to getting what you want. Just make sure that what you want is in line with God's will for you.

Luke 9:62 *Jesus told him, "Anyone who puts a hand to the plow and then looks back is not fit for the Kingdom of God."* Persistence is necessary in your walk with Christ. It is the key to consistent growth of character.

How do I develop greater persistence?

1 Chronicles 16:11 *Search for the Lord and for his strength, and keep on searching.* Continue steadfastly in prayer and seek the Lord's desire for your life.

Proverbs 4:27 *Don't get sidetracked; keep your feet from following evil.* Avoid distractions.

Galatians 6:9 *Don't get tired of doing what is good. Don't get discouraged and give up, for we will reap a harvest of blessing at the appropriate time.*
Keep your focus on the task at hand and the promise of blessing to come.

Hebrews 12:1-2 *Since we are surrounded by such a huge crowd of witnesses to the life of faith, let us strip off every weight that slows us down, especially the sin that so easily hinders our progress. And let us run with endurance the race that God has set before us. We do this by keeping our eyes on Jesus, on whom our faith depends from start to finish.*
Keep your eyes on Jesus and take courage from the examples of those who have gone before.

PROMISE FROM GOD
Matthew 7:7 *Keep on asking, and you will be given what you ask for. Keep on looking, and you will find. Keep on knocking, and the door will be opened.*

Poor / Poverty

(*see also* Financial Difficulties)

Does God really care about the poor?

Isaiah 25:4 *But to the poor, O Lord, you are a refuge from the storm, . . . a shelter from the rain and the heat.*

Psalm 40:17 *I am poor and needy, but the Lord is thinking about me right now.*

Psalm 72:12 *He will rescue the poor when they cry to him; he will help the oppressed, who have no one to defend them.*

Romans 8:35-37 *Does it mean he no longer loves us if we have trouble or calamity, or are persecuted, or are hungry or cold or in danger or threatened with death? . . . No, . . . overwhelming victory is ours through Christ, who loved us.*

Psalm 113:6-8 *Far below him are the heavens and the earth. He stoops to look, and he lifts the poor from the dirt and the needy from the garbage dump. He sets them among princes.*

God cares deeply for the poor. No matter what your circumstances, God is with you. Whether you are poor, suffering from a crippling disease, grieving over the loss of a loved one, lonely or abandoned, or living in constant danger, your greatest hope as a believer is that this condition is temporary. God promises that for all eternity you will be free from all trouble as you live with him in heaven.

What is my responsibility to the poor?

Leviticus 25:39 *If any of your Israelite relatives go bankrupt and sell themselves to you, do not treat them as slaves.*

Proverbs 19:17 *If you help the poor, you are lending to the Lord—and he will repay you!*

Proverbs 22:9 *Blessed are those who are generous, because they feed the poor.*

Isaiah 58:10 *Feed the hungry and help those in trouble. Then your light will shine out from the darkness, and the darkness around you will be as bright as day.*

God has compassion for the poor, so if you would be godly, you must have compassion for the poor. Compassion that does not reach into your checkbook or onto your "to do" list is philosophical passion, not godly passion. Helping the poor is not merely an obligation but a privilege that should bring you great joy.

PROMISES FROM GOD

Psalm 41:1 *Oh, the joys of those who are kind to the poor. The Lord rescues them in times of trouble.*

Proverbs 28:27 *Whoever gives to the poor will lack nothing. But a curse will come upon those who close their eyes to poverty.*

Prayer

(*see also* Meditation)

Why is prayer important?

Matthew 7:7-11 *Keep on asking, and you will*

be given what you ask for. Keep on looking, and you will find. Keep on knocking, and the door will be opened. For everyone who asks, receives. Everyone who seeks, finds. And the door is opened to everyone who knocks. You parents—if your children ask for a loaf of bread, do you give them a stone instead? Or if they ask for a fish, do you give them a snake? Of course not! If you sinful people know how to give good gifts to your children, how much more will your heavenly Father give good gifts to those who ask him.

There's more to prayer than just getting an answer. God often does more in your own heart through the act of prayer than he does in actually answering your prayer. As you persist in asking, seeking, and knocking, you often gain greater understanding of yourself, your situation, your motivation, and God's nature and direction for your life.

How can I know God hears my prayers?

Psalm 145:18 *The Lord is close to all who call on him, yes, to all who call on him sincerely.*
The Lord invites you to make prayer your first response rather than your last resort. He always listens to those who are honest with him.

2 Chronicles 7:14 *Then if my people who are called by my name will humble themselves and pray and seek my face and turn from their wicked ways, I will hear from heaven.*

1 Peter 3:12 *The eyes of the Lord watch over those who do right, and his ears are open to their prayers.*

Since prayer is conversation with God, you can approach God with the same love and courtesy that you bring to any relationship you value. Be humble, not arrogant. Admit your sin and seek his forgiveness.

1 John 5:14 *And we can be confident that he will listen to us whenever we ask him for anything in line with his will.*

While you may not know God's specific will for every situation, you can know that his will is to empower your obedience, to overcome evil with good, and to equip you to be his witness. Pray confidently for his power and guidance in these situations and many others, knowing that you are asking for the very things he most longs to give.

Does God always answer prayer?

Psalm 116:1-2 *I love the Lord because he hears and answers my prayers. Because he bends down and listens, I will pray as long as I have breath!*

2 Corinthians 12:8-9 *Three different times I begged the Lord to take it away. Each time he said, ". . . My power works best in your weakness."*

God always listens and responds to your prayer. But, as your loving heavenly Father who knows what is best, he does not always give you what you ask for. You can trust his answer of yes, no, or later.

PROMISES FROM GOD
James 5:16 *The earnest prayer of a righteous person has great power and wonderful results.*

Prejudice

What does God think of prejudice?

Galatians 2:12-14 *When he first arrived, he ate with the Gentile Christians, who don't bother with circumcision. But afterward, when some Jewish friends of James came, Peter wouldn't eat with the Gentiles anymore because he was afraid of what these legalists would say. Then the other Jewish Christians followed Peter's hypocrisy, and even Barnabas was influenced to join them in their hypocrisy. When I saw that they were not following the truth of the Good News, I said to Peter in front of all the others, "Since you, a Jew by birth, have discarded the Jewish laws and are living like a Gentile, why are you trying to make these Gentiles obey the Jewish laws you abandoned?"*
Any form of prejudice is inconsistent with the good news of Jesus Christ.

John 1:46 *"Nazareth!" exclaimed Nathanael. "Can anything good come from there?" "Just come and see for yourself," Philip said.*
Jesus broke the stereotypes of his time.

John 4:9   *The woman was surprised, for Jews refuse to have anything to do with Samaritans. She said to Jesus, "You are a Jew, and I am a Samaritan woman. Why are you asking me for a drink?"*
Jesus reached across lines of racial prejudice and division.

Acts 10:28   *Peter told them, "You know it is against the Jewish laws for me to come into a Gentile home like this. But God has shown me that I should never think of anyone as impure."*
God wants us to overcome our prejudices. All the things of God are available equally to all people.

How can I overcome prejudice?

1 Samuel 16:7   *Don't judge by his appearance or height. . . . The Lord doesn't make decisions the way you do! People judge by outward appearance, but the Lord looks at a person's thoughts and intentions.*

Isaiah 53:2   *My servant grew up in the Lord's presence like a tender green shoot, sprouting from a root in dry and sterile ground. There was nothing beautiful or majestic about his appearance, nothing to attract us to him.*
Stereotypes abound—prejudice against fat people, short people, skinny people, ugly people, black people, white people, yellow people, people with skin defects, bald people—the list goes on. But the real person is inside; the body is only the shell, the temporary housing. It is

wrong to judge a person by the outward appearance.

Proverbs 14:20-21 *The poor are despised even by their neighbors, while the rich have many "friends." It is sin to despise one's neighbors; blessed are those who help the poor.*

Proverbs 14:31 *Those who oppress the poor insult their Maker, but those who help the poor honor him.*

James 2:9 *But if you pay special attention to the rich, you are committing a sin.*
God condemns prejudice based on financial well being or socio-economic class. Money is not a measure of character. Simply treat others as you would like to be treated (see Matthew 7:12).

Matthew 18:10 *Beware that you don't despise a single one of these little ones. For I tell you that in heaven their angels are always in the presence of my heavenly Father.*

1 Timothy 4:12 *Don't let anyone think little of you because you are young.*

1 Timothy 5:1 *Never speak harshly to an older man, but appeal to him respectfully as though he were your own father. Talk to the younger men as you would to your own brothers.*
The Bible forbids discrimination based on age. Be attentive to the young and the old alike.

Can Christians be prejudiced against other Christians?

Romans 14:10 *Why do you look down on another Christian? Remember, each of us will stand personally before the judgment seat of God.*

Galatians 3:28 *There is no longer Jew or Gentile, slave or free, male or female. . . . You are one in Christ Jesus.*

Christians are human just like all other people and exhibit sinful human nature. But Christians are supposed to be led and controlled by the Holy Spirit and must be careful not to let feelings of prejudice control their thoughts or actions. Christians, of all people, should understand that God created all people equal in value and worth.

PROMISE FROM GOD
Colossians 3:14 *And the most important piece of clothing you must wear is love. Love is what binds us all together in perfect harmony.*

Presence of God

With all my faults and failures, how can I enter God's presence?

Ephesians 3:12 *Because of Christ and our faith in him, we can now come fearlessly into God's presence, assured of his glad welcome.*

Hebrews 10:19-22 *And so, dear brothers and sisters, we can boldly enter heaven's Most Holy Place because of the blood of Jesus. This is the new, life-giving way that Christ has opened up for us through the sacred curtain, by means of his death for us. And since we have a great High Priest who rules over God's people, let us go right into the presence of God, with true hearts fully trusting him. For our evil consciences have been sprinkled with Christ's blood to make us clean, and our bodies have been washed with pure water.*

Because of Jesus Christ's life, death, and resurrection—and your faith in him—you stand holy and blameless in the presence of God.

How can I experience God's presence for today on earth and for eternity in heaven?

John 14:23 *Jesus replied, "All those who love me will do what I say. My Father will love them, and we will come to them and live with them."*

Psalm 16:11 *You will show me the way of life, granting me the joy of your presence and the pleasures of living with you forever.*

God longs for you to enjoy fellowship with him. God's solution to the sin in your life is for you to come to him through believing and accepting Jesus' payment for your sin, turning from your sin, and obeying God. You experience God's presence daily as you look to him and for him.

What should I do when it feels like God is far away?

Joshua 1:9 *I command you—be strong and courageous! Do not be afraid or discouraged. For the Lord your God is with you wherever you go.*

Psalm 139:7 *I can never escape from your spirit! I can never get away from your presence!*

Deuteronomy 4:29 *From there you will search again for the Lord your God. And if you search for him with all your heart and soul, you will find him.*

James 4:8 *Draw close to God, and God will draw close to you.*

Faith is trusting in the fact that God is present with you regardless of the feeling that God is far away. Continue to seek God; you will find him right there.

PROMISES FROM GOD

Psalm 16:8 *I know the Lord is always with me. I will not be shaken, for he is right beside me.*

Isaiah 46:4 *I will be your God throughout your lifetime—until your hair is white with age. I made you, and I will care for you. I will carry you along and save you.*

Pressure

(*see also* Stress, Temptation)

How can I best handle pressure?

Mark 14:33-36   *He took Peter, James, and John with him, and he began to be filled with horror and deep distress. He told them, "My soul is crushed with grief to the point of death. Stay here and watch with me." He went on a little farther and fell face down on the ground. He prayed that, if it were possible, the awful hour awaiting him might pass him by. "Abba, Father," he said, "everything is possible for you. Please take this cup of suffering away from me. Yet I want your will, not mine."*

Follow Jesus' example of praying to God, seeking support from other Christians, and focusing on God's will.

Psalm 119:143   *As pressure and stress bear down on me, I find joy in your commands.*

Immerse yourself in and obey God's Word. The more you find joy in the Lord, the less you will feel stress from external pressures.

Psalm 62:1-2   *I wait quietly before God, for my salvation comes from him. He alone is my rock and my salvation, my fortress where I will never be shaken.*

Focus on God's power and ability to solve your problems.

Exodus 18:17-18, 24-26 *"This is not good!" his father-in-law exclaimed. "You're going to wear yourself out—and the people, too. This job is too heavy a burden for you to handle all by yourself. . . ." Moses listened to his father-in-law's advice and followed his suggestions. He chose capable men from all over Israel and made them judges over the people. They were put in charge of groups of one thousand, one hundred, fifty, and ten. These men were constantly available to administer justice. They brought the hard cases to Moses, but they judged the smaller matters themselves.*

Listen to godly counsel. Delegation is often an overlooked solution to the mounting pressure you feel from trying to do everything yourself.

2 Corinthians 4:8-10 *We are pressed on every side by troubles, but we are not crushed and broken. We are perplexed, but we don't give up and quit. We are hunted down, but God never abandons us. We get knocked down, but we get up again and keep going. Through suffering, these bodies of ours constantly share in the death of Jesus so that the life of Jesus may also be seen in our bodies.*

Persevere and stay focused. Pressure can draw you closer to Jesus if you ask him to help you with it.

1 Peter 5:7 *Give all your worries and cares to God, for he cares about what happens to you.*

Philippians 4:6-7 *Don't worry about anything; instead, pray about everything. Tell God what* you need, and thank him for all he has done. If you do this, you will experience God's peace, which is far more wonderful than the human mind can understand. His peace will guard your hearts and minds as you live in Christ Jesus.

Prayerfully enjoy the peace of knowing that God is in control. Let him carry your burdens to relieve the pressure and help you endure.

PROMISES FROM GOD

Psalm 55:22 *Give your burdens to the Lord, and he will take care of you. He will not permit the godly to slip and fall.*

Matthew 11:28-30 *Then Jesus said, "Come to me, all of you who are weary and carry heavy burdens, and I will give you rest. Take my yoke upon you. Let me teach you, because I am humble and gentle, and you will find rest for your souls. For my yoke fits perfectly, and the burden I give you is light."*

Problems

What are some common mistakes people make in handling problems?

Job 10:18-19 *Why, then, did you bring me out of my mother's womb? Why didn't you let me die at birth? Then I would have been spared this miserable*

*existence. I would have gone directly from the womb
to the grave.*

We sometimes doubt God's work in our lives.
When we begin to doubt God's work, we begin
to doubt God.

Genesis 16:3 *So Sarai, Abram's wife, took
Hagar the Egyptian servant and gave her to Abram
as a wife. (This happened ten years after Abram first
arrived in the land of Canaan.)*

We often impatiently take matters into our own
hands instead of allowing God to work his way.

Genesis 3:12-13 *"Yes," Adam admitted,
"but it was the woman you gave me who brought
me the fruit, and I ate it." Then the Lord God asked
the woman, "How could you do such a thing?" "The
serpent tricked me," she replied. "That's why I ate it."*

Genesis 16:5 *Then Sarai said to Abram, "It's
all your fault! Now this servant of mine is pregnant,
and she despises me, though I myself gave her the
privilege of sleeping with you. The Lord will make
you pay for doing this to me!"*

We often blame others for our self-inflicted problems and even our self-inflicted failed solutions.

Numbers 13:25-28 *After exploring the land
for forty days, the men . . . reported to the whole
community what they had seen and showed them
the fruit they had taken from the land. This was
their report to Moses: "We arrived in the land you*

*sent us to see, and it is indeed a magnificent country.
. . . But the people living there are powerful, and
their cities and towns are fortified and very large.
We also saw the descendants of Anak who are living
there!"*

We sometimes focus on the negative possibilities
of circumstance rather than the positive potential
of God at work.

G e n e s i s   1 6 : 8   *The angel said to her, "Hagar,
Sarai's servant, where have you come from, and
where are you going?" "I am running away from
my mistress," she replied.*

We sometimes yield to the temptation to run
away from our problems.

How should I learn and grow from my problems?

P s a l m   1 0 7 : 4 3   *Those who are wise will take all
this to heart; they will see in our history the faithful
love of the Lord.*

The more you see God at work in your problems,
the more you learn about his faithful, loving
character in your life. The more you learn about
what God does, the more you will want to learn
about who he is.

R o m a n s   5 : 3 - 4   *We can rejoice, too, when we
run into problems and trials, for we know that they
are good for us—they help us learn to endure. And
endurance develops strength of character in us, and*

character strengthens our confident expectation of salvation.

The more you endure life's problems, the more you see your own character strengthened. The more you become the kind of person God desires, the more you can do the kind of work God desires.

2 Corinthians 6:3-10 *We try to live in such a way that no one will be hindered from finding the Lord by the way we act. . . . We patiently endure troubles and hardships and calamities of every kind. . . . We have proved ourselves by our purity, our understanding, our patience, our kindness, our sincere love, and the power of the Holy Spirit. We have faithfully preached the truth. God's power has been working in us. . . . We serve God whether people honor us or despise us, whether they slander us or praise us. . . . Our hearts ache, but we always have joy. We are poor, but we give spiritual riches to others. We own nothing, and yet we have everything.*

The more you endure life's problems, the more you learn what is most important in life. The more you realize what is most important, the more you will put first things first.

2 Corinthians 1:8-10 *We were crushed and completely overwhelmed, and we thought we would never live through it. In fact, we expected to die. But*

as a result, we learned not to rely on ourselves, but on God who can raise the dead. And he did deliver us from mortal danger. And we are confident that he will continue to deliver us.

The more you endure life's problems, the more you learn the source of your strength and your help. When you realize the source of your strength, you rely on God to see you through life's problems.

PROMISE FROM GOD

Romans 8:28 *And we know that God causes everything to work together for the good of those who love God and are called according to his purpose for them.*

Promises

What are some of God's promises to me— his child—for today and forever?

John 3:16 *For God so loved the world that he gave his only Son, so that everyone who believes in him will not perish but have eternal life.*

Romans 6:23 *For the wages of sin is death, but the free gift of God is eternal life through Christ Jesus our Lord.*

God promises to save you if you receive the gift of his Son, Jesus Christ.

John 14:16-17 *And I will ask the Father, and he will give you another Counselor, who will never leave you. He is the Holy Spirit.*
God promises to be with you forever in the person of the Holy Spirit.

2 Peter 3:10 *But the day of the Lord will come.*
The Bible promises that Jesus will return to judge the world for its deeds.

John 14:2 *I am going to prepare a place for you. If this were not so, I would tell you plainly.*
Jesus promises to prepare an eternal home in heaven for you.

How do I know God will keep his promises?

Hebrews 6:18 *God has given us both his promise and his oath. These two things are unchangeable.*

Ephesians 1:14 *The Spirit is God's guarantee that he will give us everything he promised.*

Numbers 23:19 *God is not a man, that he should lie. He is not a human, that he should change his mind. Has he ever spoken and failed to act? Has he ever promised and not carried it through?*

2 Chronicles 6:14 *He prayed, "O Lord, God of Israel, there is no God like you in all of heaven and earth. You keep your promises and show unfailing love to all who obey you and are eager to do your will."*

Joshua 23:14 *Soon I will die, going the way of all the earth. Deep in your hearts you know that every promise of the Lord your God has come true. Not a single one has failed!*

God's promises are completely dependable and trustworthy because God himself is so. This can give you great comfort in the present, as well as assurance for the future. If the past and present verify God's dependability, the future will certainly reveal his continued dependability.

Why does it sometimes seem as if God hasn't fulfilled his promises?

2 Peter 3:8 *But you must not forget, dear friends, that a day is like a thousand years to the Lord, and a thousand years is like a day.*

Habakkuk 2:3 *But these things I plan won't happen right away. Slowly, steadily, surely, the time approaches when the vision will be fulfilled. If it seems slow, wait patiently, for it will surely take place. It will not be delayed.*

God will fulfill his promises, but sometimes his timetable is different from ours. We are called to wait and trust, confident in God's truthfulness.

What does God expect of me in regard to promises?

Numbers 30:2 *A man who makes a vow to the Lord or makes a pledge under oath must never break it.*

Proverbs 20:25 *It is dangerous to make a rash promise to God before counting the cost.*
God expects you to keep your promises.

Genesis 12:1-2, 4 *"Go to the land that I will show you. I will cause you to become the father of a great nation." . . . So Abram departed as the Lord had instructed him.*
God expects you to respond obediently in faith to his promises.

PROMISES FROM GOD

Hebrews 10:23 *God can be trusted to keep his promise.*

Galatians 3:29 *And now that you belong to Christ, you are the true children of Abraham. You are his heirs, and now all the promises God gave to him belong to you.*

Protection

Where can I find protection and safety?

Psalm 121:2-8 *My help comes from the Lord, who made the heavens and the earth! He will not let you stumble and fall; the one who watches over you will not sleep. Indeed, he who watches over Israel never tires and never sleeps. The Lord himself watches over you! The Lord stands beside you as your protective shade. . . . The Lord keeps watch over you as you come and go, both now and forever.*

Protection is directly related to the character, competence, and capability of your Protector. The Lord is unsurpassed in all areas. The Maker of heaven and earth is your personal protector. He never sleeps and never turns his attention from you. You walk securely because he guards your every step.

1 Samuel 2:9 *He will protect his godly ones.*

Job 5:19 *He will rescue you again and again so that no evil can touch you.*

Psalm 9:9 *The Lord is a shelter for the oppressed, a refuge in times of trouble.*
Though troubles and threats will find you in this fallen, rebellious world, they are not a surprise to the Lord. He never tires of saving you.

If God promises to protect me, then why do I get hurt?

Psalm 31:19 *You have done so much for those who come to you for protection.*

Daniel 3:17-18 *If we are thrown into the blazing furnace, the God whom we serve is able to save us. He will rescue us from your power, Your Majesty. But even if he doesn't, Your Majesty can be sure that we will never serve your gods or worship the gold statue you have set up.*
God promises to protect and keep safe those who love him. But the ultimate fulfillment of

this promise is in the spiritual protection of God's loving grace rather than physical protection. Like Daniel's friends, commit yourself to obeying God no matter what happens to your earthly body.

Psalm 17:8, 15 *Guard me as the apple of your eye. . . . When I awake, I will be fully satisfied, for I will see you face to face.*
The psalmist prayed to God for protection from enemies yet trusted that ultimate safety is God's salvation that leads to the hope of heaven.

Philippians 4:7 *His peace will guard your hearts and minds as you live in Christ Jesus.*
Through consistent and devoted prayer you can know the protection of God's supernatural peace.

PROMISE FROM GOD

Psalm 91:1-4 *Those who live in the shelter of the Most High will find rest in the shadow of the Almighty. This I declare of the Lord: He alone is my refuge, my place of safety; he is my God, and I am trusting him. For he will rescue you from every trap and protect you from the fatal plague. He will shield you with his wings. He will shelter you with his feathers. His faithful promises are your armor and protection.*

Quarreling

How can I avoid quarreling?

Romans 12:18 *Do your part to live in peace with everyone, as much as possible.*

Romans 15:5 *May God, who gives this patience and encouragement, help you live in complete harmony with each other—each with the attitude of Christ Jesus toward the other.*
Aim for harmony by making peace a priority in your relationships.

2 Timothy 2:24-25 *The Lord's servants must not quarrel but must be kind to everyone. They must be able to teach effectively and be patient with difficult people. They should gently teach those who oppose the truth. Perhaps God will change those people's hearts, and they will believe the truth.*

Titus 3:1-2 *Remind your people to submit to the government and its officers. They should be obedient, always ready to do what is good. They must not speak evil of anyone, and they must avoid quarreling. Instead, they should be gentle and show true humility to everyone.*

Proverbs 25:15 *Patience can persuade a prince, and soft speech can crush strong opposition.*

Proverbs 17:27 *A truly wise person uses few words; a person with understanding is even-tempered.*

207

Proverbs 15:1 *A gentle answer turns away wrath, but harsh words stir up anger.*
Your manner can be gentle, humble, kind, patient, and even-tempered. Your words can be few and gentle.

Romans 14:1 *Accept Christians who are weak in faith, and don't argue with them about what they think is right or wrong.*
Accept others, even if you don't always agree with them.

Proverbs 17:14 *Beginning a quarrel is like opening a floodgate, so drop the matter before a dispute breaks out.*

Proverbs 20:3 *Avoiding a fight is a mark of honor; only fools insist on quarreling.*
Be sensitive to mounting tensions and address issues before they escalate into quarrels.

2 Timothy 2:23 *Again I say, don't get involved in foolish, ignorant arguments that only start fights.*

2 Timothy 2:14 *Remind everyone of these things, and command them in God's name to stop fighting over words. Such arguments are useless, and they can ruin those who hear them.*

1 Timothy 1:4 *Don't let people waste time in endless speculation over myths and spiritual pedigrees. For these things only cause arguments; they don't help people live a life of faith in God.*

Titus 3:9   *Do not get involved in foolish discussions about spiritual pedigrees or in quarrels and fights about obedience to Jewish laws. These kinds of things are useless and a waste of time.*
Choose valuable topics of conversation.

Proverbs 26:21   *A quarrelsome person starts fights as easily as hot embers light charcoal or fire lights wood.*
Wisely choose the company you keep.

PROMISES FROM GOD
Matthew 5:9   *God blesses those who work for peace, for they will be called the children of God.*

James 3:18   *And those who are peacemakers will plant seeds of peace and reap a harvest of goodness.*

Rape

What is the Lord's response to rape?
Psalm 11:5   *The Lord examines both the righteous and the wicked. He hates everyone who loves violence.*

Psalm 12:5   *The Lord replies, "I have seen violence done to the helpless, and I have heard the groans of the poor. Now I will rise up to rescue them, as they have longed for me to do."*
God hates all violence; those who love violence will surely be severely judged.

Is revenge the answer to rape?

Genesis 34:2, 25 *But when the local prince, Shechem son of Hamor the Hivite, saw [Dinah], he took her and raped her. . . . Three days later, . . . Dinah's brothers, Simeon and Levi, took their swords, entered the town without opposition, and slaughtered every man there.*

Psalm 94:1 *O Lord, the God to whom vengeance belongs, O God of vengeance, let your glorious justice be seen!*

Romans 12:19 *Dear friends, never avenge yourselves. Leave that to God. For it is written, "I will take vengeance; I will repay those who deserve it," says the Lord.*

Leave revenge to God, for he is the judge of the universe. A crime must be brought to justice, but personal revenge starts an endless cycle of sin and destruction.

How can the answer possibly be forgiveness? Is forgiveness absolutely necessary?

Romans 12:21 *Don't let evil get the best of you, but conquer evil by doing good.*

Matthew 5:44 *But I say, love your enemies! Pray for those who persecute you!*

Mark 11:25 *But when you are praying, first forgive anyone you are holding a grudge against, so that your Father in heaven will forgive your sins, too.*

Matthew 18:20-21 *Then Peter came to him and asked, "Lord, how often should I forgive someone who sins against me? Seven times?" "No!" Jesus replied, "seventy times seven!"*

Christ forgave those who crucified him. Nothing is harder—or more healing—than forgiving someone who has greatly wronged you.

PROMISE FROM GOD
Psalm 10:17 *Lord, you know the hopes of the helpless. Surely you will listen to their cries and comfort them.*

Reconciliation

(*see also* Forgiveness, Refreshment, Renewal)

What does it mean to be reconciled to God?

2 Corinthians 5:19-21 *For God was in Christ, reconciling the world to himself, no longer counting people's sins against them. This is the wonderful message he has given us to tell others. . . . God made Christ, who never sinned, to be the offering for our sin, so that we could be made right with God through Christ.*

Romans 5:10 *For since we were restored to friendship with God by the death of his Son while we were still his enemies, we will certainly be delivered from eternal punishment by his life.*

Romans 5:1 *We have been made right in God's sight by faith.*

Reconciliation with God begins with a recognition that without Christ we are lost and separated from God. Through the death of the Lord Jesus Christ, God has made it possible for us to be reconciled to him. We must have faith in what Jesus Christ has done for us in order to be reconciled with God.

What does the Bible say about reconciliation between people?

Matthew 5:23-24 *So if you are standing before the altar in the Temple, offering a sacrifice to God, and you suddenly remember that someone has something against you, leave your sacrifice there beside the altar. Go and be reconciled to that person. Then come and offer your sacrifice to God.*

Being reconciled with other people is important to our relationship with God because it demonstrates how God reaches out to us to be reconciled with him.

Matthew 5:25-26 *Come to terms quickly with your enemy before it is too late and you are dragged into court, handed over to an officer, and thrown in jail. I assure you that you won't be free again until you have paid the last penny.*

Working for reconciliation with others is wise. It is important to our own health and self-preservation.

Matthew 18:15 *If another believer sins against you, go privately and point out the fault. If the other person listens and confesses it, you have won that person back.*
God wants us to resolve our differences with others because doing so promotes unity.

Genesis 33:8 *"What were all the flocks and herds I met as I came?" Esau asked. Jacob replied, "They are gifts, my lord, to ensure your goodwill."*

Proverbs 19:6 *Everyone is the friend of a person who gives gifts!*

Proverbs 21:14 *A . . . gift calms anger.*
Giving gifts can be an important part of being reconciled with other people.

Ephesians 2:14 *For Christ himself has made peace between us Jews and you Gentiles by making us all one people. He has broken down the wall of hostility that used to separate us.*
God has through Christ made a way for groups at enmity with one another to make peace and be fully reconciled.

How can I mend a broken relationship with a friend?

Colossians 3:13 *You must make allowance for each other's faults and forgive the person who offends you.*

Philemon 1:10 *My plea is that you show kindness to Onesimus.*

Reconciliation requires someone to take a first step of kindness. It requires you to look at a person in a new way.

PROMISE FROM GOD

Colossians 1:21-22   *You were his enemies, separated from him by your evil thoughts and actions, yet now he has brought you back as his friends. He has done this through his death on the cross in his own human body. As a result, he has brought you into the very presence of God, and you are holy and blameless as you stand before him without a single fault.*

Refreshment

(*see also* Healing, Reconciliation)

How can my soul be refreshed?

Psalm 90:14   *Satisfy us in the morning with your unfailing love, so we may sing for joy to the end of our lives.*
Through God's faithful, loving character.

Matthew 11:28   *Then Jesus said, "Come to me, all of you who are weary and carry heavy burdens, and I will give you rest."*
Through your relationship with Jesus.

Psalm 119:50   *Your promise revives me; it comforts me in all my troubles.*
Through God's Word.

Mark 1:35 *The next morning Jesus awoke long before daybreak and went out alone into the wilderness to pray.*
Through time spent alone with God in prayer.

Ezekiel 36:26 *And I will give you a new heart with new and right desires, and I will put a new spirit in you. I will take out your stony heart of sin and give you a new, obedient heart.*
Through obedience.

Psalm 51:2, 10, 12 *Wash me clean from my guilt. Purify me from my sin. . . . Create in me a clean heart, O God. Renew a right spirit within me. . . . Restore to me again the joy of your salvation, and make me willing to obey you.*
Through confession and repentance of sin.

Hebrews 12:11-12 *No discipline is enjoyable while it is happening—it is painful! But afterward there will be a quiet harvest of right living for those who are trained in this way. So take a new grip with your tired hands and stand firm on your shaky legs.*
Through accepting God's discipline, which brings the joy of a restored relationship with him.

2 Corinthians 4:16-17 *That is why we never give up. Though our bodies are dying, our spirits are being renewed every day. For our present troubles are quite small and won't last very long. Yet they produce for us an immeasurably great glory that will last forever!*
Through maintaining an eternal perspective.

Proverbs 11:25 *The generous prosper and are satisfied; those who refresh others will themselves be refreshed.*
Through ministering to others.

Psalm 133:1, 3 *How wonderful it is, how pleasant, when brothers live together in harmony! . . . Harmony is as refreshing as the dew from Mount Hermon that falls on the mountains of Zion. And the Lord has pronounced his blessing, even life forevermore.*
Through harmonious relationships.

How can my mind be refreshed?

Ephesians 4:22-24 *Throw off your old evil nature and your former way of life, which is rotten through and through, full of lust and deception. Instead, there must be a spiritual renewal of your thoughts and attitudes. You must display a new nature because you are a new person, created in God's likeness—righteous, holy, and true.*

Philippians 4:8-9 *And now, dear brothers and sisters, let me say one more thing as I close this letter. Fix your thoughts on what is true and honorable and right. Think about things that are pure and lovely and admirable. Think about things that are excellent and worthy of praise. Keep putting into practice all you learned from me and heard from me and saw me doing, and the God of peace will be with you.*

Through thinking on things pleasing to the
Holy Spirit.

How can my body be refreshed?

Psalm 145:16 *When you open your hand, you
satisfy the hunger and thirst of every living thing.*
Through God's provision.

Exodus 23:12 *Work for six days, and rest on
the seventh. This will give your ox and your donkey
a chance to rest. It will also allow the people of your
household, including your slaves and visitors, to be
refreshed.*
Through rest.

Proverbs 3:7-8 *Don't be impressed with your
own wisdom. Instead, fear the Lord and turn your back
on evil. Then you will gain renewed health and vitality.*
Through right living.

PROMISE FROM GOD
Psalm 119:40 *I long to obey your commandments! Renew my life with your goodness.*

Regrets

(*see also* Past)

How can I deal with the regrets of my life?

2 Corinthians 5:17 *What this means is that
those who become Christians become new persons.*

They are not the same anymore, for the old life is gone. A new life has begun!
Trust in Christ to forgive your past and give you a fresh start with God. What you regret cannot be retracted, but it can be forgiven and forgotten.

Psalm 51:1, 12 *Blot out the stain of my sins. . . . Restore to me again the joy of your salvation.*

Micah 7:19 *Once again you will have compassion on us. You will trample our sins under your feet and throw them into the depths of the ocean!*
You can deal with regrets caused by sin by confessing the sin and receiving God's forgiveness. Because God no longer holds your sins against you, you no longer have to hold them against yourself.

Ezekiel 6:9-10 *Then at last they will hate themselves for all their wickedness. They will know that I alone am the Lord.*

2 Corinthians 7:8-11 *I am no longer sorry that I sent that letter to you, though I was sorry for a time, for I know that it was painful to you for a little while. Now I am glad I sent it, not because it hurt you, but because the pain caused you to have remorse and change your ways. It was the kind of sorrow God wants his people to have, so you were not harmed by us in any way. For God can use sorrow in our lives to help us turn away from sin and seek salvation. We will never regret that kind of sorrow. But sorrow*

without repentance is the kind that results in death. Just see what this godly sorrow produced in you! Such earnestness, such concern to clear yourselves, such indignation, such alarm, such longing to see me, such zeal, and such a readiness to punish the wrongdoer. You showed that you have done everything you could to make things right.

Proverbs 14:9 *Fools make fun of guilt, but the godly acknowledge it and seek reconciliation.*
Ask yourself what God may be communicating through your regrets. God sometimes uses brokenness and remorse to bring spiritual insight and growth. Regrets that drive you to God are redemptive.

How can I avoid regrets in the future?

1 Timothy 1:19 *Cling tightly to your faith in Christ, and always keep your conscience clear. For some people have deliberately violated their consciences; as a result, their faith has been shipwrecked.*

1 Thessalonians 5:22 *Keep away from every kind of evil.*
Commit yourself decisively to a life of godliness and obedience.

Psalm 1:1-2 *Oh, the joys of those who do not follow the advice of the wicked, or stand around with sinners, or join in with scoffers. But they delight in doing everything the Lord wants; day and night they think about his law.*

Immerse yourself in Scripture and surround yourself with positive influences.

1 Samuel 15:24 *Then Saul finally admitted, "Yes, I have sinned. I have disobeyed your instructions and the Lord's command, for I was afraid of the people and did what they demanded."*
Let confidence in the Lord, not fear of people or events, determine your course of action.

Proverbs 14:29 *Those who control their anger have great understanding; those with a hasty temper will make mistakes.*
Avoid acting on impulse in the heat of anger. A hasty mistake has lasting effects.

Matthew 27:3 *When Judas, who had betrayed him, realized that Jesus had been condemned to die, he was filled with remorse.*
Consider in advance the full consequences of your decisions.

James 3:2, 5 *We all make many mistakes, but those who control their tongues can also control themselves in every other way. . . . So also, the tongue is a small thing, but what enormous damage it can do. A tiny spark can set a great forest on fire.*

Ephesians 4:29 *Don't use foul or abusive language. Let everything you say be good and helpful, so that your words will be an encouragement to those who hear them.*

Your greatest regrets are often caused by your words. Remember words once spoken cannot be taken back. Don't merely avoid hurtful words, but test your words against the standard of truthfulness, goodness, and helpfulness. If you have any thought that you might regret what you are about to say, don't speak.

PROMISE FROM GOD

Romans 4:6-8 *King David spoke of this, describing the happiness of an undeserving sinner who is declared to be righteous: "Oh, what joy for those whose disobedience is forgiven, whose sins are put out of sight. Yes, what joy for those whose sin is no longer counted against them by the Lord."*

Rejection

(*see also* Abandonment, Neglect)

I feel rejected. How will God respond to me?

Isaiah 49:15-16 *Can a mother forget her nursing child? Can she feel no love for a child she has borne? But even if that were possible, I would not forget you! See, I have written your name on my hand.*

Psalm 27:10 *Even if my father and mother abandon me, the Lord will hold me close.*

God loves you no matter what you have done or how rejected you feel. If you are feeling lonely and rejected, know that God readily welcomes you with open arms.

Genesis 16:7-8, 13 *The angel of the Lord found Hagar beside a desert spring along the road to Shur. The angel said to her, "Hagar, Sarai's servant, where have you come from, and where are you going?" "I am running away from my mistress," she replied. . . . Thereafter, Hagar referred to the Lord, who had spoken to her, as "the God who sees me," for she said, "I have seen the One who sees me!"*
God seeks you so he can bring you to himself.

Isaiah 54:17 *But in that coming day, no weapon turned against you will succeed. And everyone who tells lies in court will be brought to justice. These benefits are enjoyed by the servants of the Lord, their vindication will come from me. I, the Lord, have spoken!*

Luke 6:22-23 *God blesses you who are hated and excluded and mocked and cursed because you are identified with me, the Son of Man. When that happens, rejoice! Yes, leap for joy! For a great reward awaits you in heaven. And remember, the ancient prophets were also treated that way by your ancestors.*
God will bring you justice, mercy, and eventual reward.

Will God ever reject me?

John 6:37 *Those the Father has given me will come to me, and I will never reject them.*

222

Ephesians 3:12 *Because of Christ and our faith in him, we can now come fearlessly into God's presence, assured of his glad welcome.*

Hebrews 4:15-16 *This High Priest of ours understands our weaknesses, for he faced all of the same temptations we do, yet he did not sin. So let us come boldly to the throne of our gracious God. There we will receive his mercy, and we will find grace to help us when we need it.*

You can approach God knowing that he gladly welcomes you and will always accept you through Jesus Christ. God will never say, "Sorry, I don't have time for you," or "Sorry, don't bother me." He always listens, always hears, always loves, is always there. Even in your weakness he does not reject you but rather embraces you so that you can receive strength to be all he intended you to be. In his open arms you find a model of accepting.

How should I respond to those who reject me?

2 Corinthians 2:14-16 *Now wherever we go he uses us to tell others about the Lord and to spread the Good News like a sweet perfume. . . . But this fragrance is perceived differently by those being saved and by those perishing. To those who are perishing we are a fearful smell of death and doom. But to those who are being saved we are a life-giving perfume.*

When some reject you, they may actually be rejecting the Lord you represent. Continue to follow him and stick to his mission for you. Though others reject you, the Lord will not.

Luke 23:34 *Jesus said, "Father, forgive these people, because they don't know what they are doing."*

Acts 7:59-60 *And as they stoned him, Stephen prayed, "Lord Jesus, receive my spirit." And he fell to his knees, shouting, "Lord, don't charge them with this sin!"*

2 Timothy 4:16 *The first time I was brought before the judge, no one was with me. Everyone had abandoned me. I hope it will not be counted against them.*
Offer forgiveness for those who reject you, just as God offers forgiveness to you.

Luke 15:20-24 *So he returned home to his father. And while he was still a long distance away, his father saw him coming. Filled with love and compassion, he ran to his son, embraced him, and kissed him. His son said to him, "Father, I have sinned against both heaven and you, and I am no longer worthy of being called your son." But his father said to the servants, "Quick! Bring the finest robe in the house and put it on him. Get a ring for his finger, and sandals for his feet. And kill the calf we have been fattening in the pen. We must celebrate with a feast, for this son of mine was dead and has now returned to life. He was lost, but now he is found."* So the party began.

Rejection does not erase love. Love accepts even in the face of rejection.

PROMISE FROM GOD

Psalm 94:14   *The Lord will not reject his people; he will not abandon his own special possession.*

Relationships

How can I build healthy relationships with others?

Colossians 3:14   *And the most important piece of clothing you must wear is love. Love is what binds us all together in perfect harmony.*

Proverbs 3:3-4   *Never let loyalty and kindness get away from you! Wear them like a necklace; write them deep within your heart. Then you will find favor with both God and people, and you will gain a good reputation.*

1 Peter 2:17   *Show respect for everyone. Love your Christian brothers and sisters. Fear God. Show respect for the king.*

Ephesians 4:2   *Be humble and gentle. Be patient with each other, making allowance for each other's faults because of your love.*

The foundation of healthy relationships is love,

and the four cornerstones are loyalty, kindness, respect, and forgiveness.

What are some of the benefits of a loving relationship?

Mark 12:29-31 *Jesus replied, "The most important commandment is this: 'Hear, O Israel! The Lord our God is the one and only Lord. And you must love the Lord your God with all your heart, all your soul, all your mind, and all your strength.' The second is equally important: 'Love your neighbor as yourself.' No other commandment is greater than these."*

Proverbs 10:12 *Hatred stirs up quarrels, but love covers all offenses.*

1 Corinthians 13:4-7 *Love is patient and kind. Love is not jealous or boastful or proud or rude. Love does not demand its own way. Love is not irritable, and it keeps no record of when it has been wronged. It is never glad about injustice but rejoices whenever the truth wins out. Love never gives up, never loses faith, is always hopeful, and endures through every circumstance.*

The gifts from love include undivided and complete devotion, forgiveness, patience, kindness, love for truth, love for justice, love for the best in a person, loyalty at any cost, and belief in a person no matter what. Love prohibits jealousy, envy, pride, a haughty spirit, selfishness, rudeness, demand for one's own way, irritability, and grudges.

How can I restore broken relationships with others?

Luke 15:18 *I will go home to my father and say, "Father, I have sinned against both heaven and you."*
You may need to confess to God and to others whom you have wronged.

Matthew 18:15 *If another believer sins against you, go privately and point out the fault. If the other person listens and confesses it, you have won that person back.*
You may need to confront another in order to restore a relationship.

Ephesians 4:26, 31-32 *And "don't sin by letting anger gain control over you." Don't let the sun go down while you are still angry. . . . Get rid of all bitterness, rage, anger, harsh words, and slander, as well as all types of malicious behavior. Instead, be kind to each other, tenderhearted, forgiving one another, just as God through Christ has forgiven you.*
You must deal with your own anger in order to truly forgive others.

Genesis 50:18-21 *Then his brothers came and bowed low before him. "We are your slaves," they said. But Joseph told them, "Don't be afraid of me. Am I God, to judge and punish you? As far as I am concerned, God turned into good what you meant for evil. He brought me to the high position I have today so I could save the lives of many people. No, don't be afraid.*

Indeed, I myself will take care of you and your families."
And he spoke very kindly to them, reassuring them.
It is through forgiveness that grudges are forgotten and revenge is not an option.

Colossians 3:13 *You must make allowance for each other's faults and forgive the person who offends you. Remember, the Lord forgave you, so you must forgive others.*
God's model of forgiveness is the key to restoring relationships.

PROMISES FROM GOD

Romans 5:11 *So now we can rejoice in our wonderful new relationship with God—all because of what our Lord Jesus Christ has done for us in making us friends of God.*

Ecclesiastes 4:9-10 *Two people can accomplish more than twice as much as one; they get a better return for their labor. If one person falls, the other can reach out and help. But people who are alone when they fall are in real trouble.*

Renewal

(*see also* Healing, Reconciliation, Refreshment)

My life is a mess and I feel like I need to start over again. How can I experience renewal in my life?

Acts 3:19 *Now turn from your sins and turn to God, so you can be cleansed of your sins.*

Jeremiah 31:18 *I have heard Israel saying, "You disciplined me severely, but I deserved it. I was like a calf that needed to be trained for the yoke and plow. Turn me again to you and restore me, for you alone are the Lord my God."*

Psalm 32:3-5 *When I refused to confess my sin, I was weak and miserable, and I groaned all day long. Day and night your hand of discipline was heavy on me. My strength evaporated like water in the summer heat. Finally, I confessed all my sins to you and stopped trying to hide them. I said to myself, "I will confess my rebellion to the Lord." And you forgave me! All my guilt is gone.*

Sometimes you feel weary because you are clinging to sin and disobedience. If this is the case, then turn to God, confess your sins, and let him cleanse your heart and life. He promises to make you a brand new person! And he will give you a fresh, new start.

Ezekiel 36:26-27 *And I will give you a new heart with new and right desires, and I will put a new spirit in you. I will take out your stony heart of sin and give you a new, obedient heart. And I will put my Spirit in you so you will obey my laws and do whatever I command.*

Renewal comes from the gift of a new heart and the Holy Spirit.

Ephesians 4:22-24 *Throw off your old evil nature and your former way of life, which is rotten through and through. . . . Instead, there must be a spiritual renewal of your thoughts and attitudes. You must display a new nature because you are a new person, created in God's likeness—righteous, holy, and true.*

Colossians 3:10 *In its place you have clothed yourselves with a brand-new nature that is continually being renewed as you learn more and more about Christ, who created this new nature within you.*
Enjoy living daily in your new nature!

In what ways does God renew me?

Psalm 19:7 *The law of the Lord is perfect, reviving the soul. The decrees of the Lord are trustworthy, making wise the simple.*
God revives your soul.

Psalm 119:25 *I lie in the dust, completely discouraged; revive me by your word.*
God revives you by his Word.

Psalm 23:3 *He renews my strength. He guides me along right paths, bringing honor to his name.*
God renews your strength and promises to guide you on new pathways for your life.

Psalm 94:19 *When doubts filled my mind, your comfort gave me renewed hope and cheer.*
God renews your hope.

Psalm 119:40, 93 *I long to obey your command-ments! Renew my life with your goodness. . . . I will never forget your commandments, for you have used them to restore my joy and health.*
God restores your joy and health.

2 Corinthians 4:16 *That is why we never give up. Though our bodies are dying, our spirits are being renewed every day.*
God renews your spirit.

PROMISE FROM GOD
Psalm 51:10 *Create in me a clean heart, O God. Renew a right spirit within me.*

Rescue

From what does God rescue me?

Galatians 1:4 *He died for our sins, just as God our Father planned, in order to rescue us from this evil world in which we live.*
God rescues you from the pain and eternal conse-quences of sin. Now you are free from the hurt that comes from sin and you can experience the joy and freedom of a relationship with God.

1 Peter 2:16 *You are not slaves; you are free. But your freedom is not an excuse to do evil. You are free to live as God's slaves.*
God rescues you from the power of sin. When

you are rescued, you are free to serve God and others in love.

Colossians 1:13 *For he has rescued us from the one who rules in the kingdom of darkness, and he has brought us into the Kingdom of his dear Son.* God rescues you from the dominion of Satan. You are no longer a slave to sin, bound by the control of Satan and his temptations. You are free to live as God wants you to live. Satan no longer has control over you.

Psalm 34:4 *I prayed to the Lord, and he answered me, freeing me from all my fears.*

Hebrews 2:14-15 *Because God's children are human beings—made of flesh and blood—Jesus also became flesh and blood by being born in human form. For only as a human being could he die, and only by dying could he break the power of the Devil, who had the power of death. Only in this way could he deliver those who have lived all their lives as slaves to the fear of dying.* God rescues you from fear, even the fear of death.

1 Corinthians 10:13 *But remember that the temptations that come into your life are no different from what others experience. And God is faithful. He will keep the temptation from becoming so strong that you can't stand up against it. When you are tempted, he will show you a way out so that you will not give in to it.*

God rescues you from temptations. He does not always remove the temptations, but he always gives you the resources to be victorious over them.

Why doesn't God rescue me from all my troubles?

Psalm 34:18-19 *The Lord is close to the brokenhearted; he rescues those who are crushed in spirit. The righteous face many troubles, but the Lord rescues them from each and every one.*

Psalm 9:9-10 *The Lord is a shelter for the oppressed, a refuge in times of trouble. Those who know your name trust in you, for you, O Lord, have never abandoned anyone who searches for you.*

Isaiah 43:1-2 *But now, O Israel, the Lord who created you says: "Do not be afraid, for I have ransomed you. I have called you by name; you are mine. When you go through deep waters and great trouble, I will be with you. When you go through rivers of difficulty, you will not drown! When you walk through the fire of oppression, you will not be burned up; the flames will not consume you."*

Daniel 3:17-18 *If we are thrown into the blazing furnace, the God whom we serve is able to save us. He will rescue us from your power, Your Majesty. But even if he doesn't, Your Majesty can be sure that we will never serve your gods or worship the gold statue you have set up.*

Matthew 26:53-54 *Don't you realize that I could ask my Father for thousands of angels to protect us, and he would send them instantly? But if I did, how would the Scriptures be fulfilled that describe what must happen now?*

Daniel 12:1 *At that time Michael, the archangel who stands guard over your nation, will arise. Then there will be a time of anguish greater than any since nations first came into existence. But at that time every one of your people whose name is written in the book will be rescued.*

2 Timothy 4:18 *Yes, and the Lord will deliver me from every evil attack and will bring me safely to his heavenly Kingdom. To God be the glory forever and ever.*

Knowing God does not exempt you from troubles here on earth. He does not always prevent or remove the trouble, but he is always present in troubled times. God is clearly able to give you the strength and wisdom to overcome any and every trouble. He lovingly and sovereignly determines the timing and details of your rescue. All believers will eventually be rescued from all earthly troubles to live with him trouble-free forever.

PROMISES OF GOD

Psalm 18:19 *He led me to a place of safety; he rescued me because he delights in me.*

Psalm 91:14-15 *The Lord says, "I will rescue those who love me. I will protect those who trust in my name. When they call on me, I will answer; I will be with them in trouble. I will rescue them and honor them."*

Rest

(*see also* Peace, Security, Stress)

Why is rest so important for me?

Genesis 2:1-3 *So the creation of the heavens and the earth and everything in them was completed. On the seventh day, having finished his task, God rested from all his work. And God blessed the seventh day and declared it holy, because it was the day when he rested from his work of creation.*

Why would the omnipotent God of the universe rest following his work of creation? Surely, it wasn't because the Almighty was physically tired! A clue is that God, in ceasing from his work, called his rest "holy." God also knew that you would need to cease from your work to care for your spiritual needs. Work is good, but it must be balanced by regular attention to worship and the health of our souls. Make sure to carve out regular times for worship and spiritual refreshment. Whole life comes from holy rest.

Exodus 23:12 Work for six days, and rest on the seventh. This will give your ox and your donkey a chance to rest. It will also allow the people of your household, including your slaves and visitors, to be refreshed.

Regular, consistent, weekly rest is an important part of avoiding and recovering from burnout.

Psalm 23:1-3 The Lord is my shepherd; I have everything I need. He lets me rest in green meadows; he leads me beside peaceful streams. He renews my strength. He guides me along right paths, bringing honor to his name.

Psalm 127:2 It is useless for you to work so hard from early morning until late at night, anxiously working for food to eat; for God gives rest to his loved ones.

Accept God's provision of times for rest. Rest renews you mentally, physically, emotionally, and spiritually, thus giving you more energy for the work ahead. Rest is not only a necessity, but a gift from God you can gladly accept.

What should I do during my times of rest?

Exodus 31:13 Tell the people of Israel to keep my Sabbath day, for the Sabbath is a sign of the covenant between me and you forever. It helps you to remember that I am the Lord, who makes you holy.

Isaiah 58:13 Keep the Sabbath day holy. Don't pursue your own interests on that day, but enjoy the

Sabbath and speak of it with delight as the Lord's holy day. Honor the Lord in everything you do, and don't follow your own desires or talk idly.

Leviticus 19:30 *Keep my Sabbath days of rest and show reverence toward my sanctuary, for I am the Lord.*

Sabbath rest is to be a day dedicated to the Lord, a time when you do not pursue your own regular work. It is a time for you to remember who God is individually and corporately in worship. Rest is setting aside things that distract you from God.

Mark 6:31-32 *Then Jesus said, "Let's get away from the crowds for a while and rest." There were so many people coming and going that Jesus and his apostles didn't even have time to eat. They left by boat for a quieter spot.*

Psalm 145:5 *I will meditate on your majestic, glorious splendor and your wonderful miracles.*

Psalm 4:8 *I will lie down in peace and sleep, for you alone, O Lord, will keep me safe.*

In addition to Sabbath rest, there are times when you need emotional rest (separation from normal routine), mental rest (meditation), and physical rest (sleep). This kind of rest brings renewed energy, mental clarity, healing, and peace of mind and heart.

What is the difference between rest and laziness?

Psalm 139:3 *You chart the path ahead of me and tell me where to stop and rest. Every moment you know where I am.*

2 Thessalonians 3:11 *Yet we hear that some of you are living idle lives, refusing to work and wasting time meddling in other people's business.*

Proverbs 6:10-11 *A little extra sleep, a little more slumber, a little folding of the hands to rest— and poverty will pounce on you like a bandit; scarcity will attack you like an armed robber.*

The Bible clearly says that laziness can be a sin, while rest is refreshing. Someday you will be asked to give an account for how you spent your time here on earth. Laziness is always making excuses for why things can't get done. Rest is a reward for a job well done.

What are the dangers of not being rested?

Nehemiah 4:10 *Then the people of Judah began to complain that the workers were becoming tired. There was so much rubble to be moved that we could never get it done by ourselves.*

When you become weary, you can lose your confidence and trust in God, becoming vulnerable to temptation and to the enemy.

Ecclesiastes 1:8 *Everything is so weary and tiresome! No matter how much we see, we are never satisfied. No matter how much we hear, we are not content.*

Weariness can blur your vision and purpose.

Proverbs 30:1-2 *I am weary, O God; I am weary and worn out, O God. I am too ignorant to be human, and I lack common sense.*

Weariness can blur your perspective.

PROMISES FROM GOD

Isaiah 40:29-31 *He gives power to those who are tired and worn out; he offers strength to the weak. Even youths will become exhausted, and young men will give up. But those who wait on the Lord will find new strength. They will fly high on wings like eagles. They will run and not grow weary. They will walk and not faint.*

Matthew 11:28 *Come to me, all of you who are weary and carry heavy burdens, and I will give you rest.*

Hebrews 4:9-10 *So there is a special rest still waiting for the people of God. For all who enter into God's rest will find rest from their labors, just as God rested after creating the world.*

Revenge

Is revenge ever justified?

Leviticus 19:18 *Never seek revenge or bear a grudge against anyone, but love your neighbor as yourself.*

Revenge is forbidden in the Old Testament. Taking personal revenge is expressly forbidden by God.

1 Peter 3:9 *Don't repay evil for evil. Don't retaliate when people say unkind things about you. Instead, pay them back with a blessing. That is what God wants you to do, and he will bless you for it.* Revenge is forbidden in the New Testament. Not only is personal revenge wrong, but we are to repay evil with good.

Exodus 21:23-25 *But if any harm results, then the offender must be punished according to the injury. If the result is death, the offender must be executed. If an eye is injured, injure the eye of the person who did it. If a tooth gets knocked out, knock out the tooth of the person who did it. Similarly, the payment must be hand for hand, foot for foot, burn for burn, wound for wound, bruise for bruise.*

Deuteronomy 19:21 *Your rule should be life for life, eye for eye, tooth for tooth, hand for hand, foot for foot.*
The often quoted "eye for an eye" verses are not an excuse for, nor are they a rule for, personal revenge. This principle wasn't established to exact revenge, but rather to make sure the punishment fit the crime. If justice was to prevail, it was necessary that a person did not get off the hook for a crime, nor be punished too severely. An "eye for an eye" was actually a breakthrough for justice and fairness in ancient times because it prevented

the justice system from becoming arbitrary. There is no indication that this verse was meant to be taken literally. In fact, in Exodus 21:26-27, if a slave's eye or tooth is knocked out he can go free. The point is that the severity of the punishment should fit the severity of the crime.

Romans 12:17, 19 *Never pay back evil for evil to anyone. Do things in such a way that everyone can see you are honorable. . . . Dear friends, never avenge yourselves. Leave that to God. For it is written, "I will take vengeance; I will repay those who deserve it," says the Lord.*
God's vengeance is not to get back or get even, but to administer righteous judgment.

What are the alternatives to revenge?
1 Peter 2:21-23 *This suffering is all part of what God has called you to. Christ, who suffered for you, is your example. Follow in his steps. . . . He did not retaliate when he was insulted. When he suffered, he did not threaten to get even. He left his case in the hands of God, who always judges fairly.*
Follow Jesus' example not to retaliate. Jesus did not take revenge but fully trusted God to judge fairly.

Psalm 38:12-15 *Meanwhile, my enemies lay traps for me; they make plans to ruin me. They think up treacherous deeds all day long. But I am deaf to all their threats. I am silent before them as one who cannot speak. I choose to hear nothing, and I make no reply. For I am waiting for you, O Lord. You must answer for me, O Lord my God.*

2 Timothy 4:14 *Alexander the coppersmith has done me much harm, but the Lord will judge him for what he has done.*
Choose to refuse revengeful acts and trust God to work in his way in his time.

1 Corinthians 13:5 *Love does not demand its own way. Love is not irritable, and it keeps no record of when it has been wronged.*
Love your enemies. When you love someone, you won't take revenge on them.

Genesis 50:19-21 *Joseph told them, "Don't be afraid of me. Am I God, to judge and punish you? As far as I am concerned, God turned into good what you meant for evil. He brought me to the high position I have today so I could save the lives of many people. No, don't be afraid. Indeed, I myself will take care of you and your families." And he spoke very kindly to them, reassuring them.*
Forgive. Forgiving erases the reason for revenge.

Luke 6:27-28 *But if you are willing to listen, I say, love your enemies. Do good to those who hate you. Pray for the happiness of those who curse you. Pray for those who hurt you.*
Pray for your enemies. Prayer helps eliminate the desire for revenge.

1 Corinthians 6:7 *To have such lawsuits at all is a real defeat for you. Why not just accept the injustice and leave it at that? Why not let yourselves be cheated?*

Luke 9:52-56 *He sent messengers ahead to a Samaritan village to prepare for his arrival. But they were turned away. The people of the village refused to have anything to do with Jesus because he had resolved to go to Jerusalem. When James and John heard about it, they said to Jesus, "Lord, should we order down fire from heaven to burn them up?" But Jesus turned and rebuked them. So they went on to another village.* Accept your temporary injury and move on. Moving on leaves revenge behind.

PROMISES FROM GOD

Psalm 135:14 *For the Lord will vindicate his people and have compassion on his servants.*

Proverbs 26:27 *If you set a trap for others, you will get caught in it yourself.*

Security

(*see also* Peace, Protection, Rest)

With so much change and instability in the world, how does my faith bring security?

Proverbs 1:33 *But all who listen to me will live in peace and safety, unafraid of harm.*

Matthew 7:24 *Anyone who listens to my teaching and obeys me is wise, like a person who builds a house on solid rock.*

Psalm 40:2 *He set my feet on solid ground and steadied me as I walked along.*

When you build your life on God's truth, you have a solid foundation that will not crack under the world's pressure. The Christian's safety and security is rooted deeply in the Lord's presence. With him you can face life with great courage. Without him you stand alone.

How do I deal with my feelings of insecurity?

Ephesians 3:16-20 *I pray that from his glorious, unlimited resources he will give you mighty inner strength through his Holy Spirit. And I pray that Christ will be more and more at home in your hearts as you trust in him. May your roots go down deep into the soil of God's marvelous love. And may you have the power to understand, as all God's people should, how wide, how long, how high, and how deep his love really is. . . . By his mighty power at work within us, he is able to accomplish infinitely more than we would ever dare to ask or hope.*

Ephesians 2:10 *For we are God's masterpiece. He has created us anew in Christ Jesus, so that we can do the good things he planned for us long ago.*

Philippians 1:6 *And I am sure that God, who began the good work within you, will continue his work until it is finally finished on that day when Christ Jesus comes back again.*

Whether you feel like you measure up really doesn't matter. What makes you secure is the sure knowledge of the power of God at work within you.

PROMISES FROM GOD

Proverbs 14:26 *Those who fear the Lord are secure; he will be a place of refuge for their children.*

Psalm 63:8 *I follow close behind you; your strong right hand holds me securely.*

Self-Esteem

(see also Insignificance, Worth/Worthiness)

Am I really important to God?

Genesis 1:26-27 *Then God said, "Let us make people in our image, to be like ourselves. They will be masters over all life—the fish in the sea, the birds in the sky, and all . . . wild animals." So God created people in his own image; God patterned them after himself; male and female he created them.*

Psalm 139:13 *You made all the delicate, inner parts of my body and knit me together in my mother's womb.*

God made you in his image or likeness, the first sign of the value he places on you. No other creature on earth is made in the image of God. God made you with great skill; he crafted you with loving care. He showed how much value he places on you by the way he made you.

Psalm 139:17 *How precious are your thoughts about me, O God!*
Almighty God thinks wonderful thoughts about you all the time. He looks inside of you and sees your real value.

Psalm 139:1-3, 6 *O Lord, you have examined my heart and know everything about me. You know when I sit down or stand up. You know my every thought when far away. You chart the path ahead of me and tell me where to stop and rest. Every moment you know where I am. . . . Such knowledge is too wonderful for me!*
God values you so much that he watches over you no matter where you are or what you are doing. This truly is wonderful, too wonderful to believe. But it tells you how special he thinks you are. God cares about everything you do because he loves you so much.

1 Corinthians 6:19 *Or don't you know that your body is the temple of the Holy Spirit, who lives in you and was given to you by God?*
God values you so much that he even allows your body to become a temple in which he lives. God

does not need to live in you. He can live anywhere. But by choosing to live within you, he declares you his temple, his dwelling place.

How do I develop a healthy self-esteem?

Romans 12:3 *Be honest in your estimate of yourselves, measuring your value by how much faith God has given you.*

1 Peter 4:10 *God has given gifts to each of you. . . . Manage them well so that God's generosity can flow through you.*

Healthy self-esteem is an honest appraisal of yourself, not too proud because of the gifts and abilities God has given you, yet not so self-effacing that you fail to use your gifts and abilities to their potential.

PROMISE FROM GOD

Matthew 10:29-31 *Not even a sparrow, worth only half a penny, can fall to the ground without your Father knowing it. . . . You are more valuable to him than a whole flock of sparrows.*

Spiritual Warfare

(*see also* Enemies, Oppression, Victory)

What does the Bible say about "spiritual warfare"?

Ephesians 6:11 *Put on all of God's armor so that you will be able to stand firm against all strategies and tricks of the Devil.*
Spiritual warfare requires that you be prepared to defeat your spiritual enemy through prayer, faith, and truth.

1 Peter 5:8 *Be careful! Watch out for attacks from the Devil, your great enemy.*
Be alert at all times for the sneak attacks of the evil one.

James 4:7 *Resist the Devil, and he will flee from you.*
Resist the devil in the name and power of Jesus, and he must flee from you.

Matthew 4:4 *But Jesus told him, "No! The Scriptures say, 'People need more than bread for their life; they must feed on every word of God.'"*
When under attack by the tempter, Jesus relied on the Word of God to resist the lies of his adversary.

PROMISE FROM GOD

Ephesians 6:11 *Put on all of God's armor so that you will be able to stand firm against all strategies and tricks of the Devil.*

Strength

What can I do in God's strength?

Philippians 4:13 *For I can do everything with the help of Christ who gives me the strength I need.* There are no limits to what God can do in and through you.

Psalm 18:1-2, 29-30 *I love you, Lord; you are my strength. The Lord is my rock, my fortress, and my savior; my God is my rock, in whom I find protection. He is my shield, the strength of my salvation, and my stronghold. . . . In your strength I can crush an army; with my God I can scale any wall. As for God, his way is perfect. All the Lord's promises prove true.*

Ephesians 3:20 *Glory be to God! By his mighty power at work within us, he is able to accomplish infinitely more than we would ever dare to ask or hope.*

God's strength in you is a result of his love for you. In his strength, you have power to do things you could never do on your own. You can withstand the toughest attacks and can take the offensive to overcome your problems.

Psalm 46:1-2 *God is our refuge and strength, always ready to help in times of trouble. So we will not fear, even if earthquakes come and the mountains crumble into the sea.*

249

By God's strength you can live without fear, because God's strength drives out fear.

How can I become stronger in my faith?

John 15:4-5 *Remain in me, and I will remain in you. For a branch cannot produce fruit if it is severed from the vine, and you cannot be fruitful apart from me. Yes, I am the vine; you are the branches. Those who remain in me, and I in them, will produce much fruit. For apart from me you can do nothing.*

Your faith is strengthened as you remain in constant fellowship with God through your relationship with Jesus Christ.

1 John 2:14 *I have written to you who are young because you are strong with God's word living in your hearts, and you have won your battle with Satan.*

Your faith is strengthened by reading and studying God's Word.

Deuteronomy 11:8 *Therefore, be careful to obey every command I am giving you today, so you may have strength to go in and occupy the land you are about to enter.*

Your faith is strengthened when you obey God's call for your life and for your daily choices.

Romans 4:20 *Abraham never wavered in believing God's promise. In fact, his faith grew stronger, and in this he brought glory to God.*

Your faith is strengthened when you step out in faith. As you do, you begin to experience God's power. Faith is not stagnant, but active.

Jude 1:20 *Continue to build your lives on the foundation of your holy faith. And continue to pray as you are directed by the Holy Spirit.*
Your faith is strengthened through prayer, as you are directed by the Holy Spirit.

James 1:2-4 *Dear brothers and sisters, whenever trouble comes your way, let it be an opportunity for joy. For when your faith is tested, your endurance has a chance to grow. So let it grow, for when your endurance is fully developed, you will be strong in character and ready for anything.*
Your faith is strengthened through trials and troubles.

Romans 1:11 *For I long to visit you so I can share a spiritual blessing with you that will help you grow strong in the Lord.*
Your faith is strengthened through the mutual encouragement and accountability of other believers.

PROMISE FROM GOD
Psalm 138:3 *When I pray, you answer me; you encourage me by giving me the strength I need.*

Stress

(*see also* Pressure, Temptation)

How can I deal with stress?

2 Samuel 22:7 *But in my distress I cried out to the Lord. . . . He heard me from his sanctuary; my cry reached his ears.*

Psalm 55:22 *Give your burdens to the Lord, and he will take care of you. He will not permit the godly to slip and fall.*
Recognize that God brings true peace of heart and mind. The first step in dealing with stress is to bring your burdens to the Lord in honest prayer.

2 Corinthians 4:9 *We are hunted down, but God never abandons us. We get knocked down, but we get up again and keep going.*

Isaiah 41:10 *Don't be afraid, for I am with you. Do not be dismayed, for I am your God. I will strengthen you. I will help you. I will uphold you with my victorious right hand.*
Be aware that problems and pressures are inevitable. But even in the midst of them, God is present and invincible.

Mark 6:31 *Then Jesus said, "Let's get away from the crowds for a while and rest." There were so many people coming and going that Jesus and his apostles didn't even have time to eat.*

Make time to slow down and take a break from pressure-packed situations.

Matthew 11:28-29 *Then Jesus said, "Come to me, all of you who are weary and carry heavy burdens, and I will give you rest. Take my yoke upon you. Let me teach you, because I am humble and gentle, and you will find rest for your souls."*

Resting in Christ breaks the hold of stress. When you are yoked with him in his service, you are free from the unrealistic and destructive expectations of others that can overwhelm you. Jesus' humility and gentleness counteract the pride and irritability that fuel so much of the conflict and stress in life.

What can I learn from stress?

2 Corinthians 1:8-9 *We were crushed and completely overwhelmed, and we thought we would never live through it. In fact, we expected to die. But as a result, we learned not to rely on ourselves, but on God who can raise the dead.*

Stress exposes your human limitations so that you can discover God's limitless power and love.

Galatians 6:9 *Don't get tired of doing what is good. Don't get discouraged and give up, for we will reap a harvest of blessing at the appropriate time.*

You can learn to keep going because God has promised a rich harvest of blessing in his perfect time.

PROMISE FROM GOD

John 16:33 *I have told you all this so that you may have peace in me. Here on earth you will have many trials and sorrows. But take heart, because I have overcome the world.*

Suffering

(*see also* Hurts/Hurting, Oppression, Pain, Persecution)

Does suffering mean that God doesn't care about me?

Psalm 22:24 *For he has not ignored the suffering of the needy. He has not turned and walked away. He has listened to their cries for help.*

Psalm 23:4 *Even when I walk through the dark valley of death, I will not be afraid, for you are close beside me. Your rod and your staff protect and comfort me.*

Suffering is not a sign of God's absence; it is a fact of life in this fallen world. God is with you in the midst of life's struggles and your most intense suffering. He may not remove them from you, but he does promise to help you get through them.

John 11:33-35 *When Jesus saw her weeping and saw the other people wailing with her, he was*

moved with indignation and was deeply troubled.
"Where have you put him?" he asked them. They told
him, "Lord, come and see." Then Jesus wept.

Isaiah 53:3 *He was despised and rejected—*
a man of sorrows, acquainted with the bitterest grief.
Jesus hurts when you hurt. He not only cares,
but he also shares your sorrows.

Psalm 56:8 *You keep track of all my sorrows.*
You have collected all my tears in your bottle. You
have recorded each one in your book.
Your suffering matters to God because you
matter to God. God's care is such that not even
a single tear goes unnoticed. He knows your
every pain and will one day lead you to ultimate
victory which is the end of all suffering in
heaven.

How do I stay close to God in times of suffering?

Isaiah 43:1-2 *But now, O Israel, the Lord*
who created you says: "Do not be afraid, for I have
ransomed you. I have called you by name; you are
mine. When you go through deep waters and great
trouble, I will be with you. When you go through
rivers of difficulty, you will not drown! When you
walk through the fire of oppression, you will not be
burned up; the flames will not consume you."
Recognize that God is close to you in times of
suffering.

Psalm 126:5-6 *Those who plant in tears will harvest with shouts of joy. They weep as they go to plant their seed, but they sing as they return with the harvest.*

Romans 8:17-18 *And since we are his children, we will share his treasures—for everything God gives to his Son, Christ, is ours, too. But if we are to share his glory, we must also share his suffering. Yet what we suffer now is nothing compared to the glory he will give us later.*

Recognize that suffering is not forever. In the dark hours of the night of suffering it is hard to think of a morning of joy and gladness. But the tears of suffering are like seeds of joy. Eventually all suffering will end forever when those who believe in Jesus are welcomed into heaven.

PROMISES FROM GOD

Psalm 147:3 *He heals the brokenhearted, binding up their wounds.*

2 Corinthians 1:3-4 *All praise to the God and Father of our Lord Jesus Christ. He is the source of every mercy and the God who comforts us. He comforts us in all our troubles so that we can comfort others. When others are troubled, we will be able to give them the same comfort God has given us.*

Suicide

What does God say about suicide?

Genesis 1:27 *So God created people in his own image; God patterned them after himself; male and female he created them.*

1 Corinthians 6:20 *For God bought you with a high price. So you must honor God with your body.*
Jesus paid the ultimate sacrifice for you that you could have life. It would go against everything Jesus taught you to take your own life.

How can I deal with thoughts I have about suicide?

Matthew 28:20 *And be sure of this: "I am with you always, even to the end of the age."*
Remember that you are not alone.

Jeremiah 1:5 *I knew you before I formed you in your mother's womb. Before you were born I set you apart and appointed you as my spokesman to the world.*
When you are tempted by thoughts of hopelessness, remember that God created you and has a plan for you.

Deuteronomy 4:29 *You will search again for the Lord your God. And if you search for him with all your heart and soul, you will find him.*
Seek God, and you will find him and his purpose for you.

PROMISE FROM GOD

Jeremiah 29:11 *"For I know the plans I have for you," says the Lord. "They are plans for good and not for disaster, to give you a future and a hope."*

Support

What are some of the ways God supports me?

Psalm 94:18 *I cried out, "I'm slipping!" and your unfailing love, O Lord, supported me.*
You are supported by the very character of God—unfailing love, goodness, forgiving, merciful.

Psalm 32:8 *The Lord says, "I will guide you along the best pathway for your life. I will advise you and watch over you."*
God's guidance through answered prayer and his Word supports you.

Hebrews 1:14 *But angels are only servants. They are spirits sent from God to care for those who will receive salvation.*

2 Corinthians 1:3 *All praise to the God and Father of our Lord Jesus Christ. He is the source of every mercy and the God who comforts us.*
You are supported by God's care and comfort.

Isaiah 41:10 *Don't be afraid, for I am with you. Do not be dismayed, for I am your God. I will*

strengthen you. I will help you. I will uphold you with
my victorious right hand.

Psalm 18:35 *You have given me the shield of*
your salvation. Your right hand supports me; your
gentleness has made me great.
God's help and protection support you.

John 14:16-17, 26 *And I will ask the Father,*
and he will give you another Counselor, who will
never leave you. He is the Holy Spirit, who leads
into all truth. The world at large cannot receive him,
because it isn't looking for him and doesn't recognize
him. But you do, because he lives with you now and
later will be in you. . . . But when the Father sends
the Counselor as my representative—and by the
Counselor I mean the Holy Spirit—he will teach you
everything and will remind you of everything I myself
have told you.
You are supported by God's presence.

How can I support others?

Proverbs 27:10 *Never abandon a friend—*
either yours or your father's. Then in your time of
need, you won't have to ask your relatives for assis-
tance. It is better to go to a neighbor than to a relative
who lives far away.
You can support others by being a faithful friend.

1 Peter 3:8 *Finally, all of you should be of one*
mind, full of sympathy toward each other, loving one
another with tender hearts and humble minds.

You can support others by being sympathetic, loving, and humble.

James 5:16 *Confess your sins to each other and pray for each other so that you may be healed. The earnest prayer of a righteous person has great power and wonderful results.*
You can support others in prayer.

2 Corinthians 1:4, 6 *He comforts us in all our troubles so that we can comfort others. When others are troubled, we will be able to give them the same comfort God has given us. . . . So when we are weighed down with troubles, it is for your benefit and salvation! For when God comforts us, it is so that we, in turn, can be an encouragement to you. Then you can patiently endure the same things we suffer.*
You can support others by comforting them.

1 Thessalonians 5:11 *So encourage each other and build each other up, just as you are already doing.*
You can support others with your encouragement.

Exodus 17:12 *Moses' arms finally became too tired to hold up the staff any longer. So Aaron and Hur found a stone for him to sit on. Then they stood on each side, holding up his hands until sunset.*
You can support others through your physical assistance.

2 Corinthians 8:14 *Right now you have plenty and can help them. Then at some other time they can share with you when you need it. In this way, everyone's needs will be met.*
You can support others by practically and unselfishly meeting their needs.

PROMISE FROM GOD
Isaiah 46:4 *I will be your God throughout your lifetime—until your hair is white with age. I made you, and I will care for you. I will carry you along and save you.*

Sympathy

(*see also* Comfort, Loss, Mercy)

Does God really sympathize with me in my time of need?
Psalm 72:12-14 *He will rescue the poor when they cry to him; he will help the oppressed, who have no one to defend them. He feels pity for the weak and the needy, and he will rescue them . . . for their lives are precious to him.*

Isaiah 63:9 *In all their suffering he also suffered, and he personally rescued them. In his love and mercy he redeemed them. He lifted them up and carried them through all the years.*
No trouble comes to you without the watchful

eye of your heavenly Father seeing it and sympathizing with you. To know that he knows is the beginning of healing.

Matthew 9:36   *He felt great pity for the crowds that came, because their problems were so great and they didn't know where to go for help. They were like sheep without a shepherd.*

Hebrews 4:15   *This High Priest of ours understands our weaknesses, for he faced all of the same temptations we do, yet he did not sin.*

Hebrews 2:17-18   *It was necessary for Jesus to be in every respect like us, his brothers and sisters, so that he could be our merciful and faithful High Priest before God. He then could offer a sacrifice that would take away the sins of the people. Since he himself has gone through suffering and temptation, he is able to help us when we are being tempted.*

Hebrews 5:2   *And because he is human, he is able to deal gently with the people, though they are ignorant and wayward. For he is subject to the same weaknesses they have.*

The story of Jesus is a story of tender compassion toward those in need. Jesus became human so that he might sympathize with our every need. There is no temptation, hurt, or pain that comes into your life without touching the sympathetic heart of Jesus.

How do I become more sympathetic?

Philippians 2:1-4 *Is there any encouragement from belonging to Christ? Any comfort from his love? Any fellowship together in the Spirit? Are your hearts tender and sympathetic? Then make me truly happy by agreeing wholeheartedly with each other, loving one another, and working together with one heart and purpose. Don't be selfish; don't live to make a good impression on others. Be humble, thinking of others as better than yourself. Don't think only about your own affairs, but be interested in others, too, and what they are doing.*

Loving others is the foundation for becoming more sympathetic. Love is the lifeline of sympathy.

Exodus 23:9 *Do not oppress the foreigners living among you. You know what it is like to be a foreigner.*

Remember your own experience in the land of Egypt. Remember your own painful life experiences. It is easier to walk a difficult path with others if you have already walked the same path.

1 Samuel 1:6 *But Peninnah made fun of Hannah because the Lord had closed her womb.*

Listen with understanding and don't minimize the hurt of others.

Isaiah 58:7 *I want you to share your food with the hungry and to welcome poor wanderers into your homes. Give clothes to those who need them, and do not hide from relatives who need your help.*

263

Intentionally look for the needs of others and meet them.

PROMISES FROM GOD

Psalm 103:13   *The Lord is like a father to his children, tender and compassionate to those who fear him.*

1 Peter 3:8   *Finally, all of you should be of one mind, full of sympathy toward each other, loving one another with tender hearts and humble minds.*

Temptation

(*see also* Addiction, Pressure)

Is being tempted to sin the same as sinning?

Hebrews 4:15   *For [Jesus] faced all of the same temptations we do, yet he did not sin.*

Matthew 4:1   *Then Jesus was led out into the wilderness by the Holy Spirit to be tempted there by the Devil.*
Jesus was often tempted, yet he never gave in to the temptations. Therefore, since Jesus was sinless, being tempted is not the same as sinning. You don't have to feel guilty about the temptations you wrestle with. Rather, devote yourself to resisting them.

Do I have the power to resist temptation?

James 4:7 *Resist the Devil, and he will flee from you.*

The devil has less power than you think. The devil can tempt you, but he cannot coerce you. He can dangle the bait in front of you, but he cannot force you to take it. You can resist the devil as Jesus did: by responding to the lies of temptation with the truth of God's Word.

1 John 4:4 *The Spirit who lives in you is greater than the spirit who lives in the world.*

1 John 5:4-5 *For every child of God defeats this evil world by trusting Christ to give the victory. And the ones who win this battle against the world are the ones who believe that Jesus is the Son of God.*

You can break free from temptation when you change your focus and change your mind. Instead of thinking about your weakness, fill your mind with the promise of God's strength. In Christ you have far more power than you think. Never forget that the Holy Spirit within you is great enough to overcome any threat against you.

1 Corinthians 10:13 *But remember that the temptations that come into your life are no different from what others experience. And God is faithful. He will keep the temptation from becoming so strong that you can't stand up against it. When you are tempted, he will show you a way out so that you will not give in to it.*

Jude 1:24-25   *And now, all glory to God, who is able to keep you from stumbling, and who will bring you into his glorious presence innocent of sin and with great joy.*

Your ultimate confidence is in the Lord. As you depend more and more fully on him, he will give you the power to resist temptation.

How do I recover when I have given in to temptation?

1 John 1:9   *But if we confess our sins to him, he is faithful and just to forgive us and to cleanse us from every wrong.*

God's grace is greater than your failure. His forgiveness overcomes your sin. Satan wins when sin keeps you from turning back to God. No matter how often you fail, God welcomes you back through the love of Jesus Christ.

1 John 2:1-6   *My dear children, I am writing this to you so that you will not sin. But if you do sin, there is someone to plead for you before the Father. He is Jesus Christ, the one who pleases God completely. He is the sacrifice for our sins. He takes away not only our sins but the sins of all the world. And how can we be sure that we belong to him? By obeying his commandments. If someone says, "I belong to God," but doesn't obey God's commandments, that person is a liar and does not live in the truth. But those who obey God's word really do love him. That is the way*

to know whether or not we live in him. Those who say they live in God should live their lives as Christ did. Confess your sin to God, accept his forgiveness, and recommit to obedience.

PROMISES FROM GOD

Psalm 1:1 *Oh, the joys of those who do not follow the advice of the wicked.*

James 1:13 *And remember, no one who wants to do wrong should ever say, "God is tempting me." God is never tempted to do wrong, and he never tempts anyone else either.*

2 Thessalonians 3:3 *But the Lord is faithful; he will make you strong and guard you from the evil one.*

Terrorism

(*see also* Violence)

How can I avoid living in constant fear?

Psalm 27:1 *The Lord is my light and my salvation—so why should I be afraid? The Lord protects me from danger—so why should I tremble?*
Trusting that God is in control of the world, that he is all-powerful, and that he will one day judge all people and punish the wicked can free you from crippling fear.

Matthew 10:28 *Don't be afraid of those who want to kill you. They can only kill your body; they cannot touch your soul.*

Remembering that your eternity is secure in Christ and untouchable by terrorists can build your confidence.

Matthew 6:34 *So don't worry about tomorrow, for tomorrow will bring its own worries. Today's trouble is enough for today.*

Refuse to panic about what might happen. Fretting about the unknowable future is only debilitating. The "what if" worries are, at best, a waste of time.

Does living by faith mean I should not take precautions?

Acts 9:29-30 *[Saul] debated with some Greek-speaking Jews, but they plotted to murder him. When the believers heard about it, however, they took him to Caesarea and sent him on to his hometown of Tarsus.*

Faith is different from foolhardiness. God often gives you the wisdom to take precautions. Take such actions not because you are overcome with terror, but because you are acting wisely.

How should I pray in this time of terrorism?

Psalm 7:6 *Arise, O Lord, in anger! Stand up against the fury of my enemies! Wake up, my God, and bring justice.*

It is appropriate to be outraged by acts of terrorism and to pray that God will protect us and bring terrorists to justice.

Matthew 5:43-44 *You have heard that the law of Moses says, "Love your neighbor" and hate your enemy. But I say, love your enemies! Pray for those who persecute you.*
Pray that terrorists will find God's love and that their lives will be transformed. This is complementary, not contradictory, to the prayer that God will judge terrorists.

Matthew 6:10 *May your Kingdom come soon. May your will be done here on earth, just as it is in heaven.*
It is important to pray not just against terrorism, but for God's purposes, and to look forward to the fulfillment of God's Kingdom at the return of Jesus.

PROMISE FROM GOD

Isaiah 41:10 *Don't be afraid, for I am with you. Do not be dismayed, for I am your God. I will strengthen you. I will help you. I will uphold you with my victorious right hand.*

Thoughts

How do I make my thoughts pleasing to God?

Joshua 1:8 *Study this Book of the Law continually. Meditate on it day and night so you may be sure to obey all that is written in it. Only then will you succeed.*
Study and think about God's Word continually, and let his thoughts fill your mind.

Mark 7:20-23 *He added, "It is the thought-life that defiles you. For from within, out of a person's heart, come evil thoughts, sexual immorality, theft, murder, adultery, greed, wickedness, deceit, eagerness for lustful pleasure, envy, slander, pride, and foolishness. All these vile things come from within; they are what defile you and make you unacceptable to God."*
Get rid of evil thoughts.

Psalm 19:14 *May the words of my mouth and the thoughts of my heart be pleasing to you, O Lord, my rock and my redeemer.*
Ask God to help you have pure thoughts.

Philippians 4:8 *Dear brothers and sisters, let me say one more thing as I close this letter. Fix your thoughts on what is true and honorable and right. Think about things that are pure and lovely and admirable. Think about things that are excellent and worthy of praise.*
Fill your mind with good thoughts.

Colossians 3:2-3 *Let heaven fill your thoughts. Do not think only about things down here on earth. For you died when Christ died, and your real life is hidden with Christ in God.*
Think about heaven.

Romans 12:2 *Let God transform you into a new person by changing the way you think. Then you will know what God wants you to do, and you will know how good and pleasing and perfect his will really is.*
Let God change your thoughts.

How do my thoughts affect my actions?

Ephesians 4:17-19, 23-24 *With the Lord's authority let me say this: Live no longer as the ungodly do, for they are hopelessly confused. Their closed minds are full of darkness; they are far away from the life of God because they have shut their minds and hardened their hearts against him. They don't care anymore about right and wrong, and they have given themselves over to immoral ways. Their lives are filled with all kinds of impurity and greed. . . . Instead, there must be a spiritual renewal of your thoughts and attitudes. You must display a new nature because you are a new person, created in God's likeness—righteous, holy, and true.*

Colossians 1:21 *This includes you who were once so far away from God. You were his enemies, separated from him by your evil thoughts and actions.*

James 3:13-18 *If you are wise and understand God's ways, live a life of steady goodness so that only good deeds will pour forth. . . . The wisdom that comes from heaven is first of all pure. It is also peace loving, gentle at all times, and willing to yield to others. It is full of mercy and good deeds. It shows no partiality and is always sincere. And those who are peacemakers will plant seeds of peace and reap a harvest of goodness.*

Psalm 1:2 *But they delight in doing everything the Lord wants; day and night they think about his law.*

The seeds for your actions, both good and bad, are planted in your mind. Nurture godly thoughts and reject all perverse thoughts so that you can consistently live a life pleasing to God.

PROMISES FROM GOD

Psalm 139:2, 7, 17 *You know when I sit down or stand up. You know my every thought when far away. . . . I can never escape from your spirit! I can never get away from your presence. . . . How precious are your thoughts about me, O God! They are innumerable!*

Isaiah 26:3 *You will keep in perfect peace all who trust in you, whose thoughts are fixed on you!*

Tragedy

(*see also* Grief, Pain, Suffering)

How does God help in times of tragedy?

Psalm 55:17 *Morning, noon, and night I plead aloud in my distress, and the Lord hears my voice.*
God listens to your prayers.

Psalm 118:5 *In my distress I prayed to the Lord, and the Lord answered me and rescued me.*
God responds to your calls for help.

Psalm 46:1 *God is our refuge and strength, always ready to help in times of trouble.*
God shows himself, making his presence and his character known.

Psalm 119:43, 50, 52, 81-82, 114, 147 *Do not snatch your word of truth from me, for my only hope is in your laws. . . . Your promise revives me; it comforts me in all my troubles. . . . I meditate on your age-old laws; O Lord, they comfort me. . . . I faint with longing for your salvation; but I have put my hope in your word. My eyes are straining to see your promises come true. When will you comfort me? . . . You are my refuge and my shield; your word is my only source of hope. . . . I rise early, before the sun is up; I cry out for help and put my hope in your words.*
God comforts and guides you with his Word.

Romans 8:35-39 *Can anything ever separate us from Christ's love? Does it mean he no longer loves*

us if we have trouble or calamity, or are persecuted, or are hungry or cold or in danger or threatened with death? (Even the Scriptures say, "For your sake we are killed every day; we are being slaughtered like sheep.") No, despite all these things, overwhelming victory is ours through Christ, who loved us. And I am convinced that nothing can ever separate us from his love. Death can't, and life can't. The angels can't, and the demons can't. Our fears for today, our worries about tomorrow, and even the powers of hell can't keep God's love away. Whether we are high above the sky or in the deepest ocean, nothing in all creation will ever be able to separate us from the love of God that is revealed in Christ Jesus our Lord.
Most importantly, God continues to love you.

How can I help others cope with tragedy?

2 Corinthians 1:8-11 *I think you ought to know, dear brothers and sisters, about the trouble we went through in the province of Asia. We were crushed and completely overwhelmed, and we thought we would never live through it. In fact, we expected to die. But as a result, we learned not to rely on ourselves, but on God who can raise the dead. And he did deliver us from mortal danger. And we are confident that he will continue to deliver us. He will rescue us because you are helping by praying for us. As a result, many will give thanks to God because so many people's prayers for our safety have been answered.*
You can intercede in prayer for them.

Nehemiah 2:17 *But now I said to them, "You know full well the tragedy of our city. It lies in ruins, and its gates are burned. Let us rebuild the wall of Jerusalem and rid ourselves of this disgrace!"*
You can encourage them to follow God.

Job 2:11 *Three of Job's friends were Eliphaz the Temanite, Bildad the Shuhite, and Zophar the Naamathite. When they heard of the tragedy he had suffered, they got together and traveled from their homes to comfort and console him.*
You can comfort and console them. Sometimes your presence is better than words.

Obadiah 1:13 *You shouldn't have plundered the land of Israel when they were suffering such calamity. You shouldn't have gloated over the destruction of your relatives, looting their homes and making yourselves rich at their expense.*
You should never take advantage of tragedy in anyone's life.

Romans 15:26 *For you see, the believers in Greece have eagerly taken up an offering for the Christians in Jerusalem, who are going through such hard times.*
You can meet their physical needs in practical, compassionate ways.

PROMISE FROM GOD
Psalm 50:15 *Trust me in your times of trouble, and I will rescue you, and you will give me glory.*

Trust

What does it mean to trust God?

Romans 3:22 *We are made right in God's sight when we trust in Jesus Christ to take away our sins. And we all can be saved in this same way, no matter who we are or what we have done.*

John 3:36 *And all who believe in God's Son have eternal life. Those who don't obey the Son will never experience eternal life, but the wrath of God remains upon them.*

Trusting God means depending on Christ alone for salvation.

Psalm 62:8 *O my people, trust in him at all times. Pour out your heart to him, for God is our refuge.*

Psalm 143:8 *Let me hear of your unfailing love to me in the morning, for I am trusting you. Show me where to walk, for I have come to you in prayer.*

Trusting God is a way of life.

Ephesians 3:17 *And I pray that Christ will be more and more at home in your hearts as you trust in him. May your roots go down deep into the soil of God's marvelous love.*

Psalm 31:5 *I entrust my spirit into your hand. Rescue me, Lord, for you are a faithful God.*

Trusting God is also an ongoing process based on a personal relationship.

How do I know if I am trusting God? What are some of the signs of trusting God?

Psalm 52:7-8 *Look what happens to mighty warriors who do not trust in God. They trust their wealth instead and grow more and more bold in their wickedness. But I am like an olive tree, thriving in the house of God. I trust in God's unfailing love forever and ever.*
A thriving love relationship with God.

1 Peter 1:8-9 *You love him even though you have never seen him. Though you do not see him, you trust him; and even now you are happy with a glorious, inexpressible joy. Your reward for trusting him will be the salvation of your souls.*
Joy.

Isaiah 26:3-4 *You will keep in perfect peace all who trust in you, whose thoughts are fixed on you! Trust in the Lord always, for the Lord God is the eternal Rock.*
Peace.

Psalm 27:14 *Wait patiently for the Lord. Be brave and courageous. Yes, wait patiently for the Lord.*

Psalm 37:34 *Don't be impatient for the Lord to act! Travel steadily along his path. He will honor you, giving you the land. You will see the wicked destroyed.*
Patience.

Psalm 112:1 *Praise the Lord! Happy are those who fear the Lord. Yes, happy are those who delight in doing what he commands.*
Obedience.

Proverbs 3:5-6 *Trust in the Lord with all your heart; do not depend on your own understanding. Seek his will in all you do, and he will direct your paths.*
Guidance.

Acts 27:25 *So take courage! For I believe God. It will be just as he said.*

Hebrews 13:6 *That is why we can say with confidence, "The Lord is my helper, so I will not be afraid. What can mere mortals do to me?"*

Psalm 112:7 *They do not fear bad news; they confidently trust the Lord to care for them.*
Courage and confidence.

How can I avoid trusting in the wrong people or the wrong things?

James 1:5-8 *If you need wisdom—if you want to know what God wants you to do—ask him, and he will gladly tell you. He will not resent your asking. But when you ask him, be sure that you really expect him to answer, for a doubtful mind is as unsettled as a wave of the sea that is driven and tossed by the wind. People like that should not expect to receive anything from the Lord. They can't make up their minds. They waver back and forth in everything they do.*

Isaiah 2:22 *Stop putting your trust in mere humans. They are as frail as breath. How can they be of help to anyone?*

Proverbs 28:26 *Trusting oneself is foolish, but those who walk in wisdom are safe.*

Job 15:31 *Let them no longer trust in empty riches. They are only fooling themselves, for emptiness will be their only reward.*

Isaiah 42:17 *But those who trust in idols, calling them their gods—they will be turned away in shame.*

You need to know God so well that trusting him is a natural part of your relationship with him. As you seek his counsel with the intention of full obedience, you can trust that he will direct you according to his wisdom and his will. Consider the consequences of trusting in anyone or anything other than the one, true God. Thank God for the blessings of trusting in him alone.

PROMISE FROM GOD

Hebrews 3:14 *For if we are faithful to the end, trusting God just as firmly as when we first believed, we will share in all that belongs to Christ.*

Used/Using Others/Feeling Used

(*see also* Abuse)

How can I avoid being used by others?

Proverbs 23:1-3 *When dining with a ruler, pay attention to what is put before you. If you are a big eater, put a knife to your throat, and don't desire all the delicacies—deception may be involved.*

Isaiah 39:1-2, 5-6 *Soon after this, Merodach-baladan son of Baladan, king of Babylon, sent Hezekiah his best wishes and a gift. . . . Hezekiah welcomed the Babylonian envoys and showed them everything in his treasure-houses. . . . Then Isaiah said to Hezekiah, "Listen . . . the time is coming when everything you have . . . will be carried off to Babylon."*

Jude 1:16 *These people are grumblers and complainers, doing whatever evil they feel like. They are loudmouthed braggarts, and they flatter others to get favors in return.*

Ezekiel 45:9-10 *For this is what the Sovereign Lord says: Enough, you princes of Israel! Stop all your violence and oppression and do what is just and right. Quit robbing and cheating my people out of their land! Stop expelling them from their homes! You must use only honest weights and scales, honest dry volume measures, and honest liquid volume measures.* Don't be vulnerable; be alert, aware, and knowledgeable.

How should I respond to those who abuse me or others?

Genesis 29:15, 18, 21, 23, 25, 27, 30
*Laban said to him, "You shouldn't work for me without pay just because we are relatives. How much do you want?". . . . Since Jacob was in love with Rachel, he told her father, "I'll work for you seven years if you'll give me Rachel, your younger daughter, as my wife."
. . . Finally, the time came for him to marry her.
"I have fulfilled my contract," Jacob said to Laban.
"Now give me my wife so we can be married." . . .
That night, when it was dark, Laban took Leah to Jacob, and he slept with her. . . . But when Jacob woke up in the morning—it was Leah! "What sort of trick is this?" Jacob raged at Laban. "I worked seven years for Rachel. What do you mean by this trickery?" . . .
"Wait until the bridal week is over, and you can have Rachel, too—that is, if you promise to work another seven years for me." . . . So Jacob slept with Rachel, too, and he loved her more than Leah. He then stayed and worked the additional seven years.*
Respond with personal integrity regardless of the way others treat you.

Luke 16:2 *So his employer called him in and said, "What's this I hear about your stealing from me? Get your report in order, because you are going to be dismissed."*

1 Corinthians 5:11 *What I meant was that you are not to associate with anyone who claims to*

281

be a Christian yet indulges in sexual sin, or is greedy, or worships idols, or is abusive, or a drunkard, or a swindler. Don't even eat with such people.
Sometimes you may need to take action against the injustice, sometimes you may need to accept the injustice, and sometimes you may need to stop associating with the unjust.

PROMISE FROM GOD
Leviticus 25:17 *Show your fear of God by not taking advantage of each other. I, the Lord, am your God.*

Victory

(*see also* Enemies, Overcoming, Spiritual Warfare)

What does it mean to live a "victorious Christian life"?

1 Corinthians 15:57 *How we thank God, who gives us victory over sin and death through Jesus Christ our Lord!*

1 John 5:4 *For every child of God defeats this evil world by trusting Christ to give the victory.*
Your greatest victory is receiving God's gift of salvation, which has been won by Christ.

1 Corinthians 9:26 *So I run straight to the goal with purpose in every step.*

Ephesians 6:11 *Put on all of God's armor.*
To experience victory in the Christian life, you
must be willing to commit yourself to vigorous
spiritual training and preparation.

PROMISES FROM GOD
John 16:33 *Take heart, because I have overcome
the world.*

Violence

(*see also* Anger)

The Old Testament seems filled with violence; does God really condone such behavior?

Psalm 11:5 *The Lord . . . hates everyone who
loves violence.*

Genesis 6:11 *Now the earth had become
corrupt in God's sight, and it was filled with violence.*
God's disapproval of violence as seen in the great
Flood was his judgment against the violence of
humanity.

What does the New Testament teach about violence?

Matthew 26:52 *Those who use the sword will
be killed by the sword.*
A life of violence brings its own destruction.

Matthew 5:39 *If you are slapped on the right cheek, turn the other, too.*
According to Jesus, violence is to be replaced by a willingness to love even our enemies.

PROMISE FROM GOD
Isaiah 60:18, 22 *Violence will disappear from your land; the desolation and destruction of war will end. Salvation will surround you like city walls, and praise will be on the lips of all who enter there. . . . I, the Lord, will bring it all to pass at the right time.*

War

(*see also* Enemies, Peace, Victory)

What does God think of war?
Genesis 1:27 *So God created people in his own image; God patterned them after himself; male and female he created them.*

Psalm 116:15 *The Lord's loved ones are precious to him; it grieves him when they die.*
God created every person and God loves every person. Therefore anything that takes human life grieves God. So, even if we conclude there are times when war is permissible or necessary, remember that war should always be a last resort.

And it is wise to be careful about glorifying war and reveling in death—even the death of our enemies.

Will God ever do anything about war?

Micah 4:3   *The Lord will settle international disputes. All the nations will beat their swords into plowshares and their spears into pruning hooks. All wars will stop, and military training will come to an end.*

Psalm 46:8-9   *Come, see the glorious works of the Lord: See how he brings destruction upon the world and causes wars to cease throughout the earth. He breaks the bow and snaps the spear in two; he burns the shields with fire.*

When Jesus returns, war will be abolished forever. This is a cause for comfort and joy.

PROMISE FROM GOD

Matthew 5:9   *God blesses those who work for peace, for they will be called the children of God.*

Words

(*see also* Gossip)

Do my words really matter?

Deuteronomy 23:23 *But once you have voluntarily made a vow, be careful to do as you have said, for you have made a vow to the Lord your God.*

Joshua 9:19-20 *The leaders replied, "We have sworn an oath in the presence of the Lord, the God of Israel. We cannot touch them. We must let them live, for God would be angry with us if we broke our oath."* When you say you will do something, it should be a binding commitment. Otherwise, how can you be trusted?

Psalm 15:1-3 *Who may worship in your sanctuary, Lord? Who may enter your presence on your holy hill? Those who lead blameless lives and do what is right, speaking the truth from sincere hearts. Those who refuse to slander others or harm their neighbors or speak evil of their friends.* Your words matter to God; only those whose motives are to speak rightly can enter his presence.

James 1:26 *If you claim to be religious but don't control your tongue, you are just fooling yourself, and your religion is worthless.* Your words show what kind of person you really are.

Proverbs 11:11 *Upright citizens bless a city and make it prosper, but the talk of the wicked tears it apart.*

Proverbs 15:1 *A gentle answer turns away wrath, but harsh words stir up anger.*
Words of blessing and wicked words are both very powerful.

Proverbs 17:9 *Disregarding another person's faults preserves love; telling about them separates close friends.*
What you say makes a real difference in your relationships.

Matthew 12:36-37 *I tell you this, that you must give an account on judgment day of every idle word you speak. The words you say now reflect your fate then; either you will be justified by them or you will be condemned.*
The words you speak during your life can condemn you or justify you on Judgment Day.

What kinds of words should I speak?

Romans 15:6 *Then all of you can join together with one voice, giving praise and glory to God, the Father of our Lord Jesus Christ.*
Speak words of thanks and praise to God.

Ephesians 4:29 *Let everything you say be good and helpful, so that your words will be an encouragement to those who hear them.*
Use words that build others up.

Proverbs 15:4 *Gentle words bring life and health.*
Speak to others with gentleness.

Proverbs 25:11 *Timely advice is as lovely as golden apples in a silver basket.*
When the time is right, giving good advice can be very beneficial.

1 Peter 3:9 *Don't repay evil for evil. Don't retaliate when people say unkind things about you. Instead, pay them back with a blessing. That is what God wants you to do, and he will bless you for it.*
Use your words to bless even those who injure you.

Zechariah 8:16 *But this is what you must do Tell the truth to each other. Render verdicts in your courts that are just and that lead to peace.*
Speak truthfully.

PROMISES FROM GOD

Proverbs 10:11 *The words of the godly lead to life.*

Proverbs 10:20 *The words of the godly are like sterling silver.*

Proverbs 20:15 *Wise speech is rarer and more valuable than gold and rubies.*

Worry

(*see also* Stress)

When does worry become sin?

Matthew 13:22 *The thorny ground represents those who hear and accept the Good News, but all too quickly the message is crowded out by the cares of this life.*

Matthew 6:25-34 *So I tell you, don't worry about everyday life—whether you have enough food, drink, and clothes. Doesn't life consist of more than food and clothing? Look at the birds. They don't need to plant or harvest or put food in barns because your heavenly Father feeds them. And you are far more valuable to him than they are. Can all your worries add a single moment to your life? Of course not. . . . Why be like the pagans who are so deeply concerned about these things? Your heavenly Father already knows all your needs, and he will give you all you need from day to day if you live for him and make the Kingdom of God your primary concern. So don't worry about tomorrow, for tomorrow will bring its own worries. Today's trouble is enough for today.*

Colossians 3:2 *Let heaven fill your thoughts. Do not think only about things down here on earth.* Worry is like thorny plants—crowding your mind, heart, and life. Worry erodes your faith and robs you of the joy of anticipating God's

289

faithful provision. Worry is sin when it causes you to shift your focus from God.

What can I do with the problems that worry me?

Philippians 4:6 *Don't worry about anything; instead, pray about everything. Tell God what you need, and thank him for all he has done.*

Psalm 55:22 *Give your burdens to the Lord, and he will take care of you. He will not permit the godly to slip and fall.*

Prayer and a godly perspective drive worry from your mind and heart. Peace comes when you pray, release all your cares to the Lord, and focus your mind on the promises of God.

PROMISE FROM GOD
1 Peter 5:7 *Give all your worries and cares to God, for he cares about what happens to you.*

Worth/Worthiness

(*see also* Dignity, Insignificance, Self-Esteem)

What am I worth—what is my value to God?

Genesis 1:27 *So God created people in his own image; God patterned them after himself; male and female he created them.*

Deuteronomy 26:18 *The Lord has declared today that you are his people, his own special treasure, just as he promised, and that you must obey all his commands.*

Ephesians 2:10 *For we are God's masterpiece. He has created us anew in Christ Jesus, so that we can do the good things he planned for us long ago.*

Matthew 16:26 *And how do you benefit if you gain the whole world but lose your own soul in the process? Is anything worth more than your soul?* God made you in his own image. You are his treasure and masterpiece. Your soul is invaluable to God!

How can I keep my life focused on things of worth?

Acts 14:15 *We have come to bring you the Good News that you should turn from these worthless things to the living God, who made heaven and earth, the sea, and everything in them.*

Luke 10:42 *There is really only one thing worth being concerned about. Mary has discovered it—and I won't take it away from her.*

Philippians 3:8 *Yes, everything else is worthless when compared with the priceless gain of knowing Christ Jesus my Lord. I have discarded everything else, counting it all as garbage, so that I may have Christ.*

Psalm 119:37 *Turn my eyes from worthless things, and give me life through your word.*

Philippians 4:8 *And now, dear brothers and sisters, let me say one more thing as I close this letter. Fix your thoughts on what is true and honorable and right. Think about things that are pure and lovely and admirable. Think about things that are excellent and worthy of praise.*

Acts 20:24 *But my life is worth nothing unless I use it for doing the work assigned me by the Lord Jesus—the work of telling others the Good News about God's wonderful kindness and love.*

Keeping your eyes on God keeps your priorities and your perspective straight. When you focus on following Jesus Christ, studying the Word of God, the eternal truths of heaven, and doing God's work to build up his Kingdom, then you ensure that the focus of your life will be worthwhile.

PROMISES FROM GOD

Psalm 8:5 *For you made us only a little lower than God, and you crowned us with glory and honor.*

1 Corinthians 7:23 *God purchased you at a high price. Don't be enslaved by the world.*

Index

Alphabetical list of all topics